UNLOCKED

Being Freed from Your Dysfunctional Prison

Christina LaDonna

Cocoon to Wings
PUBLISHING

UNLOCKED

The author has shared her true story to the best of her recollection and with no intent to harm or defame others. For privacy reasons, some names, locations, and dates may have been changed.

Printed in the United States of America

ISBN: 978-1-963964-18-9 (Paperback)
ISBN: 978-1-963964-19-6 (Digital)

Library of Congress Control Number: NEED THIS NUMBER

Published by Cocoon to Wings Publishing
7810 Gall Blvd, #311
Zephyrhills, FL 33541
www.CocoontoWingsBooks.com
(813) 906-WING (9464)

Book design by ETP Creative

UNLOCKED

CONTENTS

FOREWORDS

Broken is the path that leads us to wholeness!

UNLOCKED: Being Freed from Your Dysfunctional Prison is a jeering account of the importance of coming to one's true identity, resolving personal trauma, and seeking wholeness in one's emotional journey.

In this transparent, jaw-dropping account of physical abuse, self-loathing, and eventual triumph, Christina LaDonna provides hope, help, and deliverance to those who seek freedom from childhood abuse and trauma.

—Dr. Mark T. Jones Sr.,
Pastor, Center for Manifestation, Tampa, FL

As Christina's husband, I have had an up-close, personal, and behind-the-scenes look at her journey thus far. I've had the hurtful experience of seeing her go through her insecurities, depression, and attempted suicides caused by her traumatic upbringing. But I thank God that I was able to see her get unlocked and win the fight for her deliverance and healing - through mentors, accountability, therapy, life coaching, and the love and guidance of our spiritual parents.

This book will reveal the mind of Christina as she traveled through her process and journey from victim/survivor of a cruel and occultic childhood atmosphere to being free and victorious.

—John Aydelotte

DEDICATION

I thank my heavenly Father for giving me the strength and courage not only to overcome but to be transparent while writing this book. I would not be here today if it had not been for the Lord on my side. Abba, I am grateful to have a relationship with You and to know that You have been by my side every step of the way.

To my husband, prayer-covering, biggest cheerleader, lover, and best friend. John, thank you for being by my side. Your belief and trust in God held me and our family together.

When the road was dark and gray, you stayed the course and never left my side. Thank you. Your love for me never wavered. I'm so grateful to have you. You are truly God's good and perfect gift to me. I love you!

To my children. This book is dedicated to you from a better version of your mother. I pray that my transparency and healing journey change the narratives of your lives so that you can become healed and whole adults. I love you!

In Memory of My Mommy

Thank you for being there and loving me the best you could with what you had. I have learned so much through the good and the bad. I will cherish our memories.

Dear Reader,

I am excited to embark on this journey with you. By purchasing this book, you have taken the first step and invested in your path to wholeness and freedom. As you progress through this book, expect an interactive experience. You won't simply be reading my journey; you will also embrace your own. At the end of each chapter, you will find reflections and journaling opportunities.

The difficult experiences of my life may resonate with you. You'll notice that I use the word traumas, which means a deeply distressing or disturbing experience. Trauma can be molestation, rejection, abandonment, rape, death, abuse, and the list goes on. I will touch on several types of traumas. If you feel triggered, which the Oxford Dictionary defines as "a response caused by a particular action, process, or situation," it's okay to take a break and breathe through it. Being triggered is a normal reaction if you have not dealt with your trauma areas.

Each chapter will compel you to either change or remain the same. Please know that it is harder to ignore those feelings and emotions once you have uncovered them. I hope you will consider setting aside an hour or so to engage each chapter thoroughly. This will allow you to explore your thoughts and feelings and digest what you have read. This journey takes work, but freedom is so refreshing.

Some chapters have a Trigger Warning label. The designation lets you know we are about to go into some sensitive areas. It also allows you to prepare yourself before reading. Remember, it is okay to take a break and breathe through the feelings, pain, and emotions as they arise if you need to. Reading what I have gone through can potentially cause deep-rooted emotions to arise. Go for a walk and get some fresh air. This will help you feel less closed in like if you are suffocating. Shed tears as they come. Don't hold them in or any emotion that comes with them. Releasing helps on this journey.

Please do not skip over the *Reflections* sections. They provide keys that can help you unlock your personal challenges. Some aspects might be more difficult to confront and address than others. It's perfectly acceptable to close the book and come back to it later. You may want to watch a movie, phone a friend, or even take a nap. Alternatively, you can choose to move forward but ensure you return to what you initially skipped. Each step matters, and every question is significant. Are you prepared to dive in and become unlocked? Let's begin.

Chapter 1

The Mirror-The Beginning to My Ending

"I HATE YOU! You are so weak and stupid!"

The voice was so loud in my ears, ringing and ringing nonstop like a phone. My thoughts kept beating me and repeating their disgust like a broken record.

"You are worthless! You are hopeless! Nobody even cares about you!"

The voice was like a distressing noise growing louder and louder, drowning my confidence, hope, and any self-esteem that was left. I was numb. The negative thoughts kept coming at me. Were they truth or lies? I wanted the noise to stop. In fear of losing my mind, I did the only thing I could think of to silence the voices and get a second of peace. I opened my mouth to scream, "SHUT UP!" the tears gushed down my face. But nothing came out. The words would not come. I was numb. The negative thoughts violently assaulted my confidence and self-esteem. I didn't have enough strength to command them to leave me alone,

Looking in the mirror, I saw the one making the accusations and slandering me. It was me. I saw myself in the mirror. My appearance was broken, my eyes red from crying, my hair standing on end from yanking it, trying to force the voices to stop. Sometimes, the voices sounded like Addie berating me. Sometimes, an unrecognizable but harsh and haunting voice despised me. Other times, the voices joined together like a chorus of chaos in my mind. Silence was all I wanted, but it would not come for me. The chaotic voices joined together in an evil song to drown me in insanity. I wanted to fight back, but I was drowning. The harder I tried to get out, the stronger and louder the voices became. I didn't care anymore. Wrinkled shirt and all, I had to get out of my own home. I left what was supposed to be my sanctuary, my safe place, to return to this house. This house was where it all began; now, as I sat in front of this familiar mirror, feeling broken, I ran into what I thought I was running away from. The voices, the pain, and all those feelings were stalking me and forbidding me from getting any rest or peace. In a faint whisper, I cried, sitting in Addie's house, which never heard me, "Just stop it!" I sobbed, unable to breathe through my cries.

How did I get here? Who was the shell of a person in the mirror? So many emotions were flaring up. I wanted it all to end—the noise, the pain, the tears, the voices, the hurt. I wanted SILENCE! But silence never came. *Why did she loathe me so? Why did she hide from me?*

As I sat in the dark, stale, and cold room where the Grandmother so often entertained and tortured, the smell of mothballs was in the air. The front door was a thick, heavy wooden one that sealed the room like a lid to a coffin. A full-size bed sat against the wall in the living room, a resting place of sorts. A burnt orange swivel chair made of crushed velvet material was in the corner. Its color had faded over time. Then there was the mirror; it was large, old, and square, and the wood was black with termite damage and scratches. There was other old wooden, rotting furniture in the room, but it all blurred in comparison to the burnt orange swivel chair, the mirror, and the bed I sat on. They seemed to want to participate in my desire to end my pain.

With tears still streaming down my face, I accepted their help. I dragged that ugly and worn burnt orange chair over to the bed and placed the tattered mirror in the chair before me. I wanted to see, needed to see - something. What was I looking for? I didn't really know, but I needed answers. I had to confront that which was devouring me. The pain was so great and excruciating.

I diverted my eyes from the mirror momentarily. Looking down, I realized the bottle of muscle relaxers I had refilled was in my hands, and I was gripping it with what little strength was left in me. And there was a Burger King cup with gin and juice on the floor next to my feet. At some point, after I snuck in, I poured it. I don't know if it was before I made sure no one could see in before I moved the mirror or after I moved the chair. It was almost as if that cup and bottle of pills were being illuminated like I had to acknowledge their presence. But why? My grip grew tighter on the bottle.

My mind was swirling like a snowstorm. The echo of Addie's (the Grandmother's) nasty tone and words filled everything in me and the room. Even from the grave, she scorched me with her words.

"You are nothing. Nobody wants you! Your own mother and father could not wait to get away from you. You are stupid and will never amount to anything. You are going to die here just like your mother did. You are weak!" Addie's words shouted from the grave. It was loud, piercing my ears.

I hated Addie! I hated her words! I hated what I had become. I had become what she said I would —worthless, nothing, stupid, weak, and unloved. There I sat in the coffin of doom. *What will my fate be?* Addie's words had already cursed me, condemned me, and killed me. Could I ever live anything other than the curses already spoken over me? There was no hope; my death sentence had been announced.

I hated Addie for being right; anger and rage consumed me, not just toward Addie but also toward myself. She had gotten in my head. I looked square in the mirror and started yelling at the person Addie had created. The things she had always thrown at me like weapons I had begun to use against myself. I said her words to me with as much malice as she would throw them at me.

"You are weak and stupid. You could not stand up to Addie or anybody else. You always allow people to run over you, and now you are back here, in this house, to die right where your mother died. You are going to die in the same spot, the same room, the same house-Addie's house!"

I could hear Addie in my voice. I looked in that mirror, and I saw her face. I was so tired of her voice – ever present in my life - and even more, I was tired of crying. I stared at Addie, in my reflection, then flashes of my mother came into view. *What mirror shows you something so devastating?* Her weak body. Her voice wrapped around those words, "We'll see." Paramedics doing CPR on her. It was too much. She went through so much. I could never be ...

"I hate you for not being stronger! I hate you for giving up! I hate you for not knowing how to fight for yourself! I hate you for not being a better mother! I hate you for not being a better wife. I HATE YOU! I HATE YOU! I HATE YOU!" I screamed until I was hoarse.

I could barely see her - the person in the mirror; she began to blur and disappear. Rivers of tears were pushing her away. She was all me. As she disappeared, the pain grew more intense. The more she faded, the stronger the grip on the bottle became. *What have I become?* The walls began to close in all around me. My breaths felt like I was being suffocated. *Was this indeed the end?* For years, I had been consumed by negative thoughts and emotions. I didn't know how to fight them or sort them all. Now, they had come crashing down on me like an avalanche.

> *Have you ever come face to face with yourself? In this chapter, I had a battle in the mirror between myself and my thoughts. Many times, when we are in the mirror, it's usually to mask what we believe (and see) or what others believe (and see). As you ponder this reflection, I want you to sit in front of the mirror for five minutes and write down what you see. Go deeper than your outer appearance.*

Coming Face to Face - Reflection

> *Finally, believers, whatever is true, whatever is honorable and worthy of respect, whatever is right and confirmed by God's word, whatever is pure and wholesome, whatever is lovely and brings peace, whatever is admirable and of good repute; if there is any excellence, if there is anything worthy of praise, think continually on these things [center your mind on them and implant them in your heart].*
>
> *Philippians 4:8 (AMP)*

One of the keys to getting unlocked is mirror reflections. Have you ever stopped and sat (or stood) before a mirror, staring at yourself while speaking aloud about how much you love yourself and how proud you are of what you have accomplished? Your answer may be no. I had struggled with this for years before getting help. This was a technique that I was taught in different therapy, counseling, and coaching sessions. Sometimes, when we look in the mirror, we judge ourselves based on how we look, feel, or what someone else has said about us. Now, we have internalized the negativity and adopted the sentiments of that person. But it's all a LIE! So, how do we change the narrative of the lie that we have taken root in our minds and now feels embedded in our emotional DNA? We must change the narrative of the negative into the positive.

For example:

- *"You are stupid" becomes "I am smart."*
- *"You are weak" becomes "I am strong."*
- *"I hate you" becomes "I love you."*

Take some time to sit before a mirror and be transparent with yourself. What thoughts come to your mind about you? What has been said to or about you that weighs on your mind, causing heaviness? Make a list and journal your feelings here in the space provided. Then, go back and write the opposite of the negative things that were said. Begin using these as your new daily affirmations. Embed them deep down in your spirit. Your thought process can change, and it will.

Now that you have reframed the negative narrative and written down what is positive and possible, you can return to the mirror and speak those positive affirmations into your life. How do you feel now? Was it challenging, or was it easy? Why or why not?

Will this become a new daily commitment for you? Will you commit to affirming yourself for six weeks to experience real change? I want you to write five to seven new affirmations of your own here. Remember to journal how you feel after committing to six weeks of positive affirmations. What has changed? Also, check in with yourself in three weeks, your halfway mark. At the end of your six weeks, look at what you wrote at the halfway mark versus the end mark. Do you see any difference?

Chapter 2

The Beginning—Foundation or Fracture

My mind was racing and all over the place, and that's when I saw it. It was a flashback, more like an out-of-body experience in a crazy movie at the same time. I was there, and yet, not there. In the back room of the house, this same house, on the other side, at only three days old at the time, I was taken by Addie to the back room where it was dark and weird music was playing. Such an eerie feeling came over me as this experience unfolded. I wanted to run, but I was being drawn into the room. The music was merely sounds, no words, only weird sounds. A candle was lit, and Addie held me up and chanted something. I was sitting in the present while looking into the past. It reminded me of the scene in the movie, "The Lion King," where they presented Simba to the animals. The words were inaudible at first; other words were unclear to me, but I could understand certain words she kept saying repeatedly. As I kept watching, I realized I was watching a dedication ceremony. Who was she presenting me to? What was happening? What was I witnessing? Little did I know this was the first piece to the puzzle of doom and dysfunction that would somehow become my life; the unveiling of different pieces would happen over the years.

As the memories continued, I saw my mother, Donna, who was only a teenager when she had me. She was encouraged to live her own life and for me to be raised by my grandmother. She was 15 when I was born. I mean, what could she possibly know about raising a baby; she was still a baby herself. When Addie took over raising me, she probably was relieved. The Grandmother took over everything concerning me, so Mommy went on about her life, in a sense, because that was the plan. Well, Addie's plan was at least to have her own child and raise it how she wanted. She was still in the house with us for a few years, but Addie did everything for me. My mom attempted to be there for me, but her mom would block her attempts as if she was not wanted and as if she was not my mommy. She would try to take me with her if she was going somewhere or doing things for me, but Addie always said no.

Addie could never have children of her own, so she and her husband adopted my mommy when she was around one or two years old.

When I came along as a newborn baby, she couldn't wait to get a hold of me. She continued blocking my mommy from me for years until Mom finally left and eventually married a guy in the military to get away from Addie. She didn't realize that when she left Addie, she also left me. Or maybe she did realize it but chose to be free from Addie's grasp. In her decision to be free, I was held hostage. I felt trapped and alone. I wanted my mommy. At times, it felt like she loved me, but that's not what Addie would tell me.

I was told all these awful things about my mommy by the one raising me in an attempt for me to love and honor her more. (I guess.) She would say my mother couldn't wait to get away from me. That she didn't really want me and only had me because she couldn't get another abortion. I would be sad and cry sometimes, only for Addie to fake comfort me and say that she wanted me.

I believed the lies I was being told for a while, but I still wanted my mother. Mommy and I did have some fun times. We would laugh together and dance around the house. She took me to the park when she was allowed to. We played games at home, and she had the best hugs.

It seems like the more that I asked for my mother, the more horrific the stories of how she didn't want me got. Having to hear repeatedly that your mother wanted to abort you rather than have you hurt. Sometimes, Addie would say that she tried to do things to have a miscarriage since she could not have the abortion. As a child, why would I believe that she was lying? I mean, she loved me, right? It was all brainwashing for what was in store for me. Addie wanted to make sure she had my allegiance to her and no longer to my mommy. The more hurt that I felt by the stories that she told me about her, she was able to come in and save the day, as if she rescued me from a horrible fate - a mother who didn't want me. I felt so broken and lost without my mommy. I would remember snippets of things we did together that made me smile momentarily. The thought of being with my mommy for the short time we had caused me to smile. But then that smile would always turn to a frown, and a small, lonely teardrop would fall because it was all a memory and not a reality. *Did my mother really not want me? Was I a bad girl?*

Well, at least I had Harold. He was my dad, who would come around occasionally, pick me up, and take me to his mom's (Grandma Gladys') house. Grandma Gladys was sweet and loving, not like Addie at all. They were like night and day. Addie was a dose of daily poison in words, actions, and intentions. Addie was the bully kid who would tear down your Lego ® castle and laugh while she did so. That was not who my dad's mother was at all.

My Grandma Gladys was a beautiful chocolate woman whose smile could light up a room. She was short in stature and didn't play about her family. She baked the most delicious cakes I had ever tasted, and her food was amazing. My Grandma Gladys had a gentle spirit about her; I don't recall her cursing or yelling at us. But if you got in trouble, then you knew that she would be on your behind, and even in that, you knew that she loved you, so it didn't feel malicious or evil. I didn't get to spend as much time with Grandma Gladys as I would have liked to. But each time I got the chance to be around her, I always felt loved. Addie made sure that I was limited in the amount of time I could spend with my dad's side of the family. I was mostly allowed to go over there on holidays, like Thanksgiving and Christmas. Sometimes, she would allow me to spend the weekend with my cousins, but not very often.

Looking back at the negative things Addie had to say concerning my dad and his side of the family, I can see where it caused me to be guarded and how it caused conflict and separation between me and my paternal family. She would say they didn't like me and didn't really accept me because they never liked my mother and were being nice to me because of my dad. She would give me these talks right before I was picked up to go over there. Then, I would be nervous and sad. Maybe she did this so I wouldn't ask to stay over. Maybe she did this to keep control so I wouldn't choose my dad over her. My dad enlisted in the Army soon after I started believing Addie's version of how he felt about me, so I saw him and talked with him even less than before. With him gone, I couldn't ask him if what she was saying was true. When we did talk, she was right there watching me and listening to our conversations.

My dad had six siblings, so I had plenty of cousins, but we were not particularly close. They were around each other more and got to play with each other often. I was only there during the holidays.

I felt like the black sheep of the family - like I never quite fit in. They would tease me and sometimes make fun of me. It hurt my feelings and made me believe what Addie had been telling me was true. My aunts and uncles seemed nice, but I wanted to get along and play with the kids. Being an only child, I craved time with other kids. At times, it felt like I was watching a softball game from outside the fence, longing to play. My hands would grip the fence tightly as I watched them play together, having fun and laughing. I did my best to fight the thoughts to get past the teasing at times so I could play. Sometimes, it worked; other times, it didn't. If I went back inside, the adults would ask why I wasn't playing with them. And when I said they were teasing me, then they got in trouble. They were forced to play with me at times, but that didn't make it any better. I just wanted to be included, liked, and fit in. I didn't want them to be forced to play with me. I wanted them to genuinely want to play with me and be nice to me. I wanted them to love me.

No matter what, the one person I always remained close to was my granddaddy, Ulysses. He was my dad's father, but he was no longer with Grandma Gladys. He lived in a run-down house, some would call it a shack, on the same street that Addie's house was on but at the other end of the street near the railroad tracks. My granddaddy had a lot of dogs surrounding his home so that no one would break in. Although I'm not sure what they were going to find, but he made sure that his place was secure. There were grapefruit and orange trees in his yard, too. Sometimes, he would let me pick fruit all by myself if they hung low enough. My grandaddy Ulysses was cool like that; he allowed me to do things to feel more independent as I grew up.

Since he lived so close to me, I was able to see him more often. To get to his house, I had to cross the main street and then go down. My granddaddy Ulysses was of medium height and had a slender build. His hair was gray and a little curly, but he always wore a hat. Whether he was working or sharply dressed for church, the man wore a hat. He had baseball caps and gentleman's hats for church and dressy occasions. And don't let the condition of his home fool you because he could dress. My granddaddy would come out of his house dressed sharp —like a king or royalty. His hat and shoes always matched his handkerchief. If he had a blue suit on with gray pinstripes, the hat would be gray with some blue in it, as well as the handkerchief and the shoes. He was a gentleman. I felt closer to him than anyone on my dad's side of the family.

I had friends that I played with on that side of the street, too, so anytime I was allowed to go and play with them, I would stop by Granddaddy's house. I never went inside, though. We would talk and laugh in his yard outside the house. He always asked me how I was doing, made sure that I was doing well in school, and that I knew he loved me.

My dad came home from the military after being away for some years. I still didn't see him often unless he came to see me. He didn't live close to me like his daddy did. Addie still kept close reins on me, controlling how much time I could spend with him. I still missed my mommy, but my dad was back home. My grandaddy always said my dad loved me. It felt hard to believe due to what Addie would tell me and him not being around. But I knew my grandaddy wouldn't lie to me. Still, his absence, even when he came home, left me confused. My confusion grew when my dad decided to leave again.

My dad decided to move to California to pursue a career in music. Once again, I was told my parent didn't want me, and that was why he moved across the country to get away from me, as if I didn't exist. This is what Addie told me, so that is what I felt: abandoned, rejected, and non-existent. How could the two people who created me leave and abandon me as if I were trash, some discarded thing? I mean, come on, he moved way across the country, and my mom left and got married to someone else in another state and didn't come back for me. *Was I that horrible?* My own mother and father didn't want me. The feeling of brokenness from being rejected and abandoned was almost unbearable. I always wanted to be a daddy's girl, but that would never happen. He came to visit from time to time. It was nice but always too short of a visit. I also had to share him with my cousins and his siblings. I just wanted my daddy all to myself. When he would leave, my heart would hurt all over again. Like a dagger being plunged in deep. It didn't help that Addie would twist the knife in my heart a little deeper each time he left with harsh words about how he didn't want me and just came to see me out of guilt. *What was wrong with me? Was I a terrible child?* No one seemed to want me, well, at least not my parents. Many times, I felt like a bad child or a bad person in general the way that Addie beat me. Like any child, I did things to get into trouble at times, but the beatings that I received were horrible. Most children get spanked with a belt. I was beaten with an extension cord. Why did she hate me? Did I deserve all of this?

To my amazement, some hope eventually came. About four years later, my mommy finally came back home to help out around the house when my granddaddy Sylvester, her dad, got sick. I was so happy and excited to have my mommy back home with me. We went to the park and the movies, made ice cream floats together, and danced around the house to "oldies" music while eating chocolate chip cookies and drinking Coca-Cola. But soon, the happiness and excitement turned into confusion and chaos. There was a power struggle between the grandmother and my mommy over who I was supposed to listen to and obey. The tug of war for control between her and the grandmother was awful. I wanted to escape it all. For several years, I was confused, and I would go to see the counselor at my elementary school weekly because I was so unhappy and stressed. I had sessions with her from first grade up until about fourth grade. The counseling sessions were my safe place; they were my happy place, well, they were until the counselor called my house. Why? Why did the counselor have to call the house to help me out? Talking to her weekly was enough. I was able to release the built-up anger, sadness, resentment, and pain that I felt concerning my parents leaving me and the things Addie would say about them. But no! She had to be Ms. Helps-a-lot and ruin everything with that stupid phone call.

Of course, I got into trouble because you don't go putting your business out in the streets. Addie always said, "What happens in this house stays in this house." What a volatile cocktail those words are. And unknowingly, that cycle gets repeated, and what is broken stays broken because it all stays in the house. It then piles up until there is no more room; the pressure is so intense and so great, and at some point, it all explodes without warning. After getting my behind "tore up" for putting her business out in the streets, as Addie told me, I stopped going to the counselor. I didn't trust her anymore, or anyone for that matter. The things I was not allowed to say in the house or even ask at home, I was allowed to vent and question with the counselor. Once that trust was betrayed, all the secrets, hurt, and pains stayed in that house once again.

> *Where were you fractured? For me, it was both of my parents leaving me, resulting in the pangs of abandonment and rejection. It took time and help, but I was able to get resolution. As you begin this reflection, think about who may have abandoned and rejected you and how that has shaped you and your relationships.*

Where was Your Fracture? - Reflection

Who was the person who abandoned you and/or rejected you? Whether it is factual or perceived in your mind, our mind can make things a reality even if they are not. It could have been your mother, father, grandmother, or grandfather. When they left, there was a hole, a void in you that you felt could not be filled.

When you reflect on them and consider who you are today, do you see a reflection of yourself? Even the things we hate or say we won't do, unconsciously, we imitate and become.

After honest introspection, do you have any of their character traits? If you answered yes, it's okay because you can change it. It's not too late to become who you desire to become. Also, take a moment to reflect on your past and current relationships. Do they have a pattern of abandonment and rejection? Or have you left them prematurely to avoid the feeling? (Example: I will leave them before they can leave me or before I get hurt again.)

Now that you can see the pattern, what will you do differently? You may need some help healing those fractures, which is perfectly fine. Getting a life coach or even seeking a therapist to help is a good step in healing those fractures. Also, if the person (or persons) is alive, make an effort to talk to them and tell them how you feel. If they are no longer alive, write them a letter expressing how you felt and how you feel right now. Once you are finished and ready to truly let it go, burn the letter in a safe place, and as the ashes begin to fly away, picture all the hurt, pain, and rejection flying away as well. Give yourself permission to release it all and begin the healing.

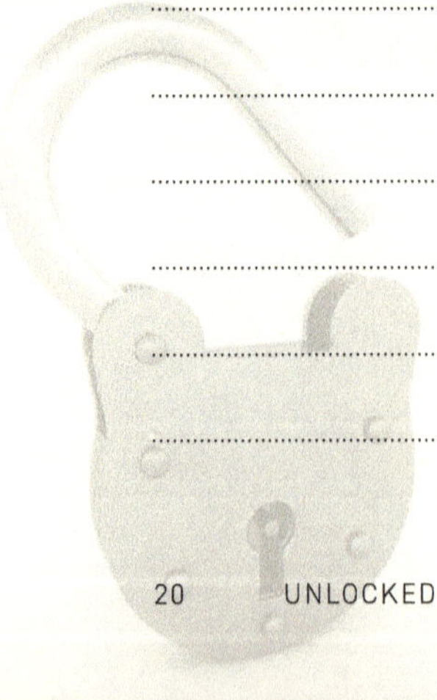

Chapter 3

Lost a Great Love

Addie's husband, Granddaddy Sylvester, "Ves," as he was affectionately called, loved me dearly and spoiled me like he did my mommy. He worked a lot, so I was mostly home with "the grandmother." He did his best to make up for the hurt that I felt from not having my parents at home with me. I don't know if he knew what Addie would tell me about them. He was my superhero because he would save me from the evil villain, his wife. Whenever she yelled at me about something or tried to spank me, and he was around, he would always stop her. She didn't like that one bit.

He, like my granddaddy Ulysses, loved me unconditionally; he may not have been my daddy, but he was the closest and best thing next to him. If I did something wrong, he didn't make me feel horrible or beat me, but he would talk to me and explain to me that the choices I made were not good ones, and he walked me through what I needed to do next time. The few times that he did spank me were not mean or malicious, like when the grandmother spanked me. Addie hated it; she accused him of loving me more than her. There was always a lot of arguing between them. War was always going on in our house. But it was heaven when he and I were together watching wrestling or me watching him do handyman stuff. No arguing, no fussing, no fighting, just fun, laughter and love. Funny how I didn't realize until I was too deep in the trauma of rejection that my grandfathers were there to show me what genuine love could be. When you live wrapped in pain, you don't see it.

The only peace I had with him was when she was not around, or I would tag along with him when he went to work. He owned a handyman business, so I could tag along with him sometimes and wait in the truck while he serviced his clients. On one of my tag-along days, he brought me a snack, a coloring book, crayons, and a toy to play with. I was happy to be with him and even more excited about my toys, so I didn't mind sitting in the truck while he worked. I watched him walk toward the house that he was going to work in. He had parked his truck across the street and several houses down from the customer's home.

It was super-hot, so Grandaddy rolled down the windows enough for me to get some air but not enough for anyone to get in. I sat in his white Chevy pickup truck, played with my toys, and had my snack. It seemed like he was taking forever, but I could not get out of the truck, or I would get into trouble. At some point, I curled up on the seat and napped until I heard a noise that woke me from my sleep. As I peered through the truck's back window, I saw my grandaddy coming out of the house. "Finally," I thought until it happened. He was standing in the doorway of the house, and I could see a lady in a skimpy sleep outfit standing in front of him. I saw her kiss him. I jumped, and when I did, it shook the truck. I was scared and confused. What had I just seen? Who was that lady? Did they see me see them?

My granddaddy started walking back to the truck; I quickly closed my eyes and pretended to be still asleep. When he opened the door and called my name, I stretched and said, "Yes sir," making sure to sound sleepy.

He asked with a sharp stare, "Did you see anything?"

"No, grandaddy, I was sleeping. Can I please use the bathroom?"

I quickly changed the subject so we could hurry and leave. He semi-smiled and said, "Okay." He glanced back before we drove off. I was probably six or so at the time, but I was old enough to know what I did see was wrong. I loved my grandaddy more than Addie, so I never told her. I was scared that she would make him leave me.

Despite his shortcomings, my granddaddy was an amazing man; he worked hard and made me feel like a princess. He would always make time for me. That is what my grandmother hated most: that he was available for me. Losing him was a devastating blow. As much as I loved him, I was also angry with him for dying and leaving me with her. I was angry at God, too, for taking him away from me.

Have you ever watched someone you love die? Words cannot truly describe how you feel.

I watched him die a horrific death from lung cancer. I would help to take care of him when he got sick. Anything to be close to him and not near her. The day that he died is still vivid in my mind. My mommy had left to go to work; I was playing in my room and had gotten hungry. Technically, I was supposed to be cleaning my room. I came downstairs and asked for lunch. The grandmother began to fix my food; it was hotdogs. It's funny how certain things stick out in your memory, like the aroma of the pot of boiling water that the hot dogs rested in on the stove. I was hungry and ready to eat, but they were not ready yet. I danced around anxiously and then got scolded by Addie for moving too much. "Fine," I exclaimed in my head as I walked away. I went to check on my granddaddy in the room she had set up for him alone. The room felt extra cold that day and somewhat dark. The vibe was off; something was wrong, and I knew it, so I stayed close. He was trying to be cheerful for me, but I saw past it to the pain in his eyes.

He wanted something to eat and drink. I went to tell the grandmother, but she snapped at me and said he had to wait. I was mad! If I were big enough, I would have fixed it for him. I was only seven then and definitely not allowed in Addie's kitchen. He was sick, and she was not being nice. I heard him coughing, so I went back to check on him, and he was coughing so hard. I started to shake because the look on his face was terrifying. It seemed as if he couldn't breathe. I hurried down the hall from the room to the kitchen to tell Addie. It was not that far of a distance, but it seemed like forever at that point.

She said, "Hold on!"

Now, that was the point I wanted to cuss. Honestly, I probably did in my head. I ran back to the room with my granddaddy, and the coughing worsened. Then, without warning, he began coughing up blood. It violently rushed from his mouth and his nose. I screamed! Addie came running in to see what had happened while fussing at me about screaming in the house. Her eyes grew wide in horror at the sight of him violently coughing up blood. She tried to get him to stop but it kept erupting in a continued forceful flow.

She told me to run and get my other granddaddy, Ulysses, who lived down the street. I was frozen, and my feet felt like lead stuck in cement; I didn't move. She yelled at me to "Go!" I broke free from my frozen state and ran as fast as I could out of the house and down the street, crying all the way. I was so distraught as I was running that when I came to the main street, I didn't stop to look both ways. I barreled across the street, running bare feet to get Ulysses. Thank God no cars were coming. When I reached him, he was mowing the grass near his house. I was out of breath and sobbing. He could barely understand me.

I finally got out what was happening, and he returned with me immediately. My granddaddy Ves, my superhero, was still coughing up blood. We needed help! Where were they? Turns out Ulysses had to call 911 when he got there. Addie never did. They tried to get me to leave the room, but I didn't want to leave him.

"NO!" I cried, "Granddaddy, please be okay, please."

Addie had called the next-door neighbor over, and she dragged me onto the porch. I was crying and protesting. I wanted my granddaddy. What was taking the ambulance so long to get there? I waited on the porch for what seemed like forever. As we waited, Addie brought my hot dog out to me and said, "Eat." I was visibly upset and still crying, and this lady wanted me to eat a hot dog. Are you kidding me?

The next-door neighbor, Ms. Jenny, urged me to eat it, but I was too shaken. I dropped it on the ground while attempting to take a bite. Addie scolded me for wasting food. Ms. Jenny protested for me, but Addie started yelling and was about to unleash her wrath on her when we heard the sirens. Finally, they had shown up! I maneuvered my way back in behind the ambulance crew so I could see. But it was too late. The last of the blood that had been rushing out like a raging waterfall had finally become a trickle, and my granddaddy slumped over. I screamed like never before. Ulysses grabbed me and took me back outside. He held me so tight that I could barely breathe. This was not happening. My heart broke into what felt like a million pieces that day. Just like that, he was gone.

Horror over? No! After they had taken my grandaddy's body away, Addie made me help her clean up his room. The room where he had just died. It was filled with the stench of blood. The entire mattress and box spring were saturated with his blood. How could so much blood come from one person? There was blood on the pillows, blanket, sheets, bed, floor, and wall. She didn't want help from Ms. Jenny, even though she insisted several times she would help her. I don't know what was more traumatizing, watching him die a horrific death or having to clean it up afterward. She was actually trying to save the blood-soaked mattress. We dragged his bed outside in the backyard piece by piece to clean it. I was still shaking as I tried to clean the blood-stained pillows. My mommy finally got there, and she and the neighbors had to convince Addie to throw it all away and allow me to go back inside so I didn't see any more.

I was numb. I was lost. I felt hopeless. What was I going to do now? The one person who loved me and understood me was gone. I blamed Addie. How could she be so heartless to not see about him sooner? Why didn't she call 911 sooner herself? He could have been saved. He should have been saved. She let him die! I hated her for that. How can you say you love someone and won't do everything you can to save them? Was it true? Did she let him die, or was it his time to go? I will never know, but my life changed forever that day. Love seemed to be locked behind bars again.

I was able to go far back into my childhood and share some painful moments. While they were happening, I felt that I would not be able to get over them. My granddaddy, Ves, protected me and was the closest one I had to a father since my birth father had moved away and was not present daily in my life. Who for you was that constant, dependable person who was abruptly taken away from you, and you felt as though you could not go on? As you prepare to do your reflection, think about them.

Do you Remember? - Reflection

How far back can you remember from your childhood? What horrible or painful thing happened that you can still vividly remember and not shake? Take a moment to breathe and go back in your mind. Write what you can remember.

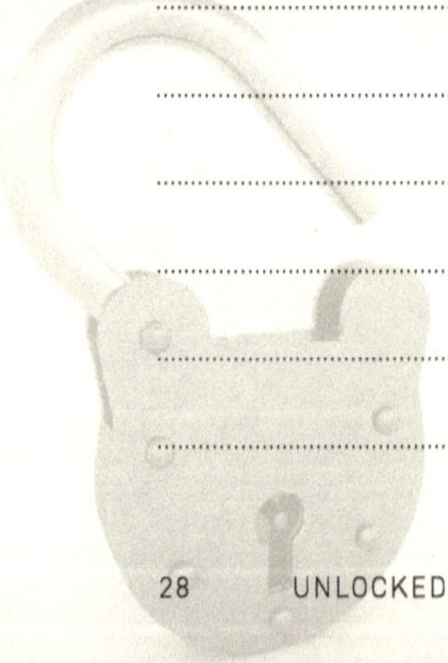

Who was that one person who you loved dearly and who loved you in return? They were the ones who could make you feel like everything would be okay. When they left your life, how did you deal with it? Have you been able to move on since they have been gone? (This person could have died or left your life in another manner). Losing a great love is hard, but you can get through it, live, and love again. Allow yourself to grieve them if you have not. There is no time limit on how long you grieve. However, make sure that it is healthy grieving. Don't shut the world out. Go out and do the things that made you feel good when you were with the person you are mourning. Learn to make new memories in their honor. What things can you begin to do that you have not done already?

Do you still feel the same pain and hurt now as you did all those years ago? What are you doing to deal with that pain? Has it affected how you live and think today? What would you like to change concerning how you feel about those thoughts and feelings?

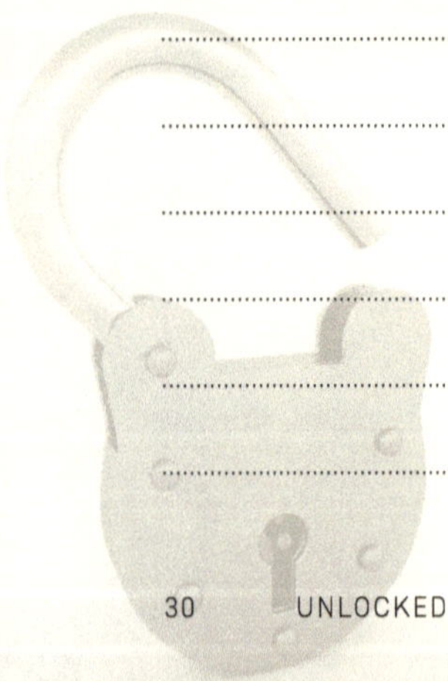

Chapter 4

Addie "The grandmother"- Sweet or Salty?

Who established your foundation? For me, it was Addie, the grandmother. She played a pivotal role (though it was negative and disparaging) in my development and growth mentally, physically, emotionally, and spiritually. In chapter two, I shared that Addie adopted my mother as a toddler. She could never have children of her own. My mother got pregnant and had me at the age of 15, so Addie raised me as if I were her daughter also and not her granddaughter. She thought that adopting a child would somehow save her troubled marriage, which was revealed in secret family gossip. Initially, it helped some; they no longer were looking at separating, but soon, her anger grew when it seemed her husband, Sylvester, loved their daughter, Donna, more than her. Tensions would arise again. A child was not the answer to their troubled marriage, yet they stayed together for the sake of their daughter. Mommy would tell me years later that watching a loveless marriage all those years caused her to look for love in all the wrong places.

Addie was an attractive woman of medium height, about 5'5", bright-skinned, with jet-black hair. She was a hard worker. Her mouth was sharp and matter-of-fact. She said what she said and meant what she said, no matter how you felt about it. She didn't back down from much of anything and would cuss you out if she felt the need, no matter who you were or where you were. Maybe her harshness came from her mother, who had abandoned her and did not want her; she was left to be raised by her grandmother. She was a hustler at heart. She did what she needed to and had to so she could have money in her pockets to pay her bills. No matter what that meant. She always had male friends, even when my grandaddy was alive. They mostly came around when he was not home. She gambled and "ran numbers," which meant she served as a neighborhood bookie, and people would wage bets on what number would come in from different gambling events. She sold moonshine, held house parties, played lotto, and was the candy lady in the neighborhood. Did I mention she whored and was a pimp?

Addie thought she had the world fooled. She believed people thought she was sweet and loving, a grandmother who gave gifts, baked cookies, and shared wisdom. But those who really knew her knew the truth. Her outer appearance was different from her inner personality. Those she would help out occasionally thought she was so sweet. She could look like the sugar and spice mature woman role. But she would help them and then talk about them like a dog, bragging about how they were down and out, and she did this and that for them. Well, as the old saying goes, "You can't judge a book by its cover." I knew all her friends' personal business. As a child, I couldn't care less about who was sleeping with who, their financial problems, or marriage issues. As I became a teenager, her friends also began to know my business or at least Addie's version of what I was doing. How did I know? Well, they were always too eager to tell me what I was doing wrong or how disappointed they were. Little did they know I knew all their dirt and chose not to reveal it.

Oh, and the sharp, slick mouth she had, yeah, I inherited some of that. I heard her cuss the pastor out. I heard her cuss a few people out in church, too. My mommy and I were included in her cursing. She was no respecter of persons; she didn't care who you were. If she felt you warranted it, you got it, no matter the time, place, or who was around.

The Relics

She always had some relics (something that has survived from the past, such as an object or custom) placed or lying around the house. She would often speak of having good luck charms. She had a rabbit's foot keychain, wishbones above the doorways, a four-leaf clover pressed into the coffee table, and countless other things. Some of her relics, I found out much later, were demonic. Statues, symbols, black rocks, and glasses with water and pennies in them. She also had a big Bible on the table in the living room, but I never saw her open it. It was for show; she bragged about how she was such a Christian. As I got older and began to know more about God for myself, I questioned the so-called good luck charms. I asked Addie, "If we are Christians, shouldn't our trust be in God and not pieces of material?" Well, I got cussed out, needless to say, for even asking the question. I would also get cussed out and hit if I touched her Bible - the big one. I remember it was extra big and white, with gold letters on the outside and gold on the page edges. Looking back, some of the things in there were confusing and hard to pronounce. Now that I know the Bible for myself, I know that it was not a regular Bible. Not God's version, anyway. It had many of the same scriptures as a regular Bible, but there were other words and symbols added. I once went to a scripture that I knew by heart and even that one had extra words that were written differently. This gossiping, pimping, sharp-tongued, cursing grandmother was practicing witchcraft. She was an actual spell-casting witch. Later, I would learn it was a Masonic bible that included spells. She was part of a secret society. She believed that certain things brought her luck with money, men, and power. Not only did she have these items around the house, but I would sometimes hear her praying to them. It was more of a chant of certain phrases. If she was angry, she went to the big Bible on the table, grabbed it, and went into her back room. Music would begin to play low, and she would begin chanting aloud. It was a bit creepy, so I would go to my room so I didn't have to hear it. Technically, I was not supposed to be listening to what was going on anyway.

Addie always told me stories about how people were after her or my mom. Once, she told me about a lady who gave my mom a sandwich mixed with green flies for her to eat when she was a little girl. That was her reasoning for not allowing me to go places or eat at other people's houses because they were also after me because they secretly hated her and how good God was to her. She even said that some of the people were in the church. As a child growing up, why would I believe that she would lie to me or mislead me in any way? I must be honest; there were times when she could be sweet and loving, but they were so rare it's hard to remember most of them. My dominant experiences with her were when she was behaving mean, evil, and scary. Those experiences could appear almost daily, especially for a child growing up in Addie's world, where the story changed according to how she felt.

I was an adventurous child; I wouldn't say bad (well, sometimes maybe), but the beatings that I got were the worst. They were supposed to be discipline, but I later found out her style of beating was abuse. See, Addie's way of discipline was to make me strip butt naked, tie my hands and feet with old strips of cloth, have me lay across the bed, and beat me with a thick extension cord. She would cuss me out, accuse me, and berate me as she beat me. Every word came with a crash of the extension cord all over my body. I would cry, scream, and flap around until I was able to set myself free, and at some point, she would stop. I still cringe sometimes, even now thinking about it. Once the beating was over, she would then place me in a bathtub of Epsom salt to help heal the welts on my body faster. Talk about adding insult to injury. The sting from the salt on my broken and bruised skin was excruciating at times. After that, she would rub me down with alcohol; this was to aid in the quick healing as well, or so she said. "You better not tell nobody," she would say.

I had to wear long-sleeved shirts and long pants to cover the bruises until they healed. It was so painful. Why did she hate me so? I honestly thought everyone got disciplined like that. She would threaten me never to tell anyone about it. I was so scared; who was I going to tell? The mind games, manipulation, and control were so strong I didn't know what to do or think except for what she told me. Years later, after conversing with someone,

I found out that what she was doing was wrong, and I could call the police on her. I may have been close to 12 or 13 by then. But I was too scared to call the police on Addie. Who would save me if I did that, and how would I do that?

I was never shown how to dial the operator in case of an emergency or call 911. Nope. That's like giving your prisoner the blueprint to the jail where you have them locked up. Being controlled and manipulated is another form of witchcraft. Your will is no longer your own but what the other person dictates. You may know or feel that something is not right, but you are powerless to change it. So, you go along with the flow like a puppet on a string. Changing your dynamics from a faulty foundation to a firm one can be hard, but it still can be done.

> *Who established your foundation? For me, it was the grandmother. She set my core beliefs, values, and character. At the time, I didn't think I had a choice but to change what I had come to know. As you begin this reflection, consider who raised you and helped set your beliefs, character, and how you do things.*

Who Set Your Foundation? - Reflection

> *The word which came to Jeremiah from the Lord: "Arise and go down to the potter's house, and there I will make you hear My words." Then I went down to the potter's house, and saw that he was working at the wheel. But the vessel that he was making from clay was spoiled by the potter's hand; so he made it over, reworking it and making it into another pot that seemed good to him. Then the word of the Lord came to me: "O house of Israel, can I not do with you as this potter does?" says the Lord. "Look carefully, as the clay is in the potter's hand, so are you in My hand, O house of Israel. At one moment I might [suddenly] speak concerning a nation or kingdom, that I will uproot and break down and destroy; if that nation against which I have spoken turns from its evil, I will relent and reverse My decision concerning the devastation that I intended to do. - Jeremiah 18:1-8 (AMP)*

Who was the person who laid the foundation for your beliefs and core values? It could have been your mother, father, grandmother, grandfather, aunt, or uncle -basically, the individuals who raised you. When you reflect on them and compare them to who you are today, do you see a reflection of yourself? This reflection can be either positive or negative, prompting a moment of self-introspection.

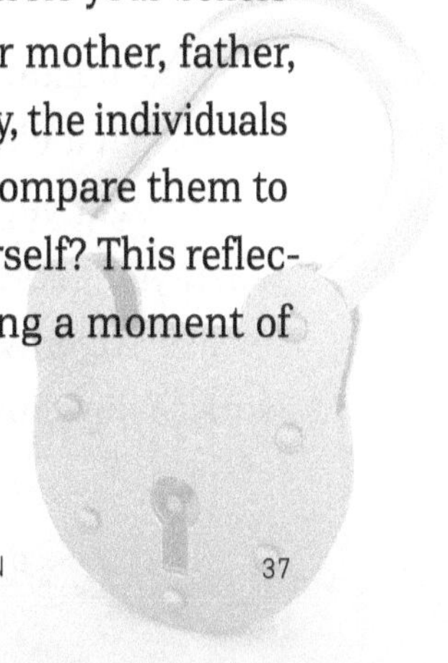

Ask yourself: Do you believe you have a solid foundation to build upon or continue with? If not, what steps will you take to bring about change?

You don't have to remain the same or continue being a carbon copy of who raised you. You can change. What lessons have you learned from the good, the bad, and the ugly)? Step back and separate yourself from the relationships. Step away from them as Momma, Daddy, or Grandma. Look at them as a person unattached to you. What did they deal with growing up that may have shaped them negatively and caused them to shape you the same way? When you get to the root of the issue, you can begin to heal and release anger. We all have root issues. Are you willing to do the work to dig yours up?

During this journaling time, separate the title from the person and deal with them as a person (grandmother-Addie, mother-Donna). Who are they? Where did they come from? Who raised them? Were they abused or mistreated? Dig and discover who and what set their foundation. You may begin to have compassion for them instead of resentment. As you get revelation, write down those new thoughts and feelings concerning them.

Now that you have a different perspective, what can you do to change how you do things and set a new foundation for yourself?

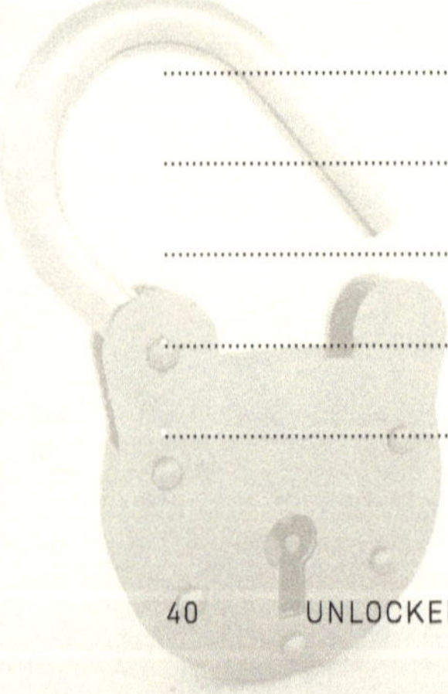

Chapter 5

No Protection-All Alone

"Uncle, No!"

He was only called my "uncle," they all were, though there was no family relationship. This uncle attempted to go further than the others did. I was only about eight years old and had to do as I was told. The grandmother had many male friends; they all were my uncles; at least, that was what Addie told me I was supposed to call them. Some of these same uncles were around when my granddaddy was still alive. I would see them from time to time at the house when he was not at home. At that time, they just spoke to me. After he died, they became way more than friendly, hugging and kissing me. Not like a quick hello kiss, but several kisses on my face and neck. Then, they wanted me to sit on their laps all the time. It was cool initially because they would give me a dollar or two to get candy from the store. Then, it got weird and uncomfortable. If I complained to them or Addie or resisted, I got into trouble with Addie.

One morning, while I was still in my night clothes, a thin, almost sheer nightgown, Addie called me downstairs to speak to my other uncle.

"Hello," was all I said.

He replied, "Good morning, darling! Come give me a hug."

Reluctantly, I walked toward him to hug him. I didn't like his hugs because he was always touching me all over, and I didn't like it, so I tried to pull back.

He quickly grabbed my hand and said, "Come sit on my lap, and I will tell you a story."

I tried to say no, but Addie quickly pushed me toward him and said, "Be nice and let your uncle tell you a story."

Shaky and uncomfortable, I was placed on the uncle's lap. He decided to play horsey first to get me to calm down and feel more at ease. He pretended like his leg was the horse and bounced me all around, making funny noises so that I would laugh. I soon came to realize it was a setup.

I laughed, he laughed, and then he began to tickle me. It was cool at first, but then he started to tickle me in areas that were not funny. Not funny at all. I squirmed to get free. I didn't like this feeling and wanted Addie, but where did she go?

"Shh! Be quiet; it's okay," he whispered in my ear.

"I want my grandma...," but he placed his hand over my mouth before I could finish my sentence.

"I don't want to hurt you or your grandma, so be quiet and just sit here," he exclaimed. I was scared, and I did not want him to hurt her. I mean, she was not particularly nice, but she was still my grandmother by this point and all I had left. His hands kept roaming all over my tiny body. His breath was hot and heavy, and he smelled of beer when he spoke to me; it made me nauseous. I tried to clamp my legs shut, but he was too big and powerful for me to fight off. Imagine a giant bodybuilder and a small rag doll. As an eight-year-old, that was what the comparison of me to him felt like. He was bigger than me, with strong muscles and big hands. Trying to fight my way out of his grasp felt useless. Silent tears fell from my eyes as he continued to touch me. Then, all of a sudden, a sharp, thick pain jabbed me in my private area. I could not control it, and I screamed, "Ow! That hurts. Please stop!!"

I heard the rustling of feet coming toward us in the back room from the front; it was the grandmother. She had left me alone with him when he began playing horsey with me.

"What's going on?" she yelled. But she was yelling at me, not him. I was crying harder by that time.

I didn't even mind being yelled at because she had just saved me. "What is going on? Why are you screaming and crying?" Her tone was irritated, as if she was being disturbed by something else important.

I was scared, but I opened my mouth and said, "He hurt me. He put something in my pee pee, and it hurts." The tears were still streaming down my face.

"She is lying; I was just playing with her," he replied anxiously. His eyes were stretched wide as if he had just been caught stealing with his hand in the cookie jar. He looked back and forth between us, not sure of what to say next. What happened next was unbelievable.

The grandmother slapped me down to the ground and said, "You fast-tail heifer, I will deal with you later." As I tried to get up and run, she grabbed a strap and hit me with it a few times. She swung the strap wildly and hit me wherever, not caring at all where it landed. Even though it stung and hurt, it was far better than what I had just endured. The uncle had jetted to the front of the house, and she ran after him. He had saved me from getting beat more. *What just happened?* He was hurting me, and I got yelled at and slapped to the ground. *How?*

Hurt, beaten, and broken, I crawled under the dining room table to hide and cry. It seemed extra dark in that back room alone, hiding under the table. I could see the burglar bars that made up the front part as a wall and doorway to the room and the thick orange curtains to conceal what was in the room. I felt as though I was in a prison with no way of escape. Staring back at me was the chair. The chair where the uncle had just hurt me. It was taunting me. In the silence of the room, I could almost hear the chair mocking me, laughing at me about what had just happened. Like mean kids on the playground after you have gotten knocked down by the mean bully. Laughing and pointing and calling you names. That was how the chair was making me feel at that moment. I could not move.

I heard shouting coming from the front part of the house. It was the grandmother and the "uncle." I covered my ears at first to muffle the sounds. My tiny body was in so much pain. Not just from what the uncle did to me but the beating that Addie gave me before chasing after him. The arguing continued for what seemed like forever. Too afraid to move, I curled up under the table in that dark, desolate room and cried. Under the table became my cave of sorts. I was scared but safe for the moment.

I would face the truth years later: so much of my trauma began with the 8-year-old scared, hiding in the corner, under the table. She had been molested, abused, and beaten. She was frightened because the very one who was supposed to have protected her was the one who was abusing her and prostituting her to her male friends. *How could Addie have done such a thing? I was a child.* But when I spoke up because he was hurting me and had gone further than he was supposed to by trying to penetrate me, I got into trouble, not him. That incident that morning created a horrible imprint on that child and on what I encountered over the years.

Eventually, I found out what all the screaming was about between the uncle and the grandmother. She was getting paid by several men to let me sit on their laps and play inappropriately with me. Have you heard of R. Kelly's song "Bump n' Grind?" See, the uncle didn't see anything wrong with a little bump and grind-it didn't matter that I was a child, apparently. He called me "baby" and wanted my body next to his.

Well, I was the foreplay, and she was the rest. This is why I called her a pimp. She pimped her own granddaughter out for money.

Because I messed up her money, she beat me again as if I had done something wrong, yet she put me in that position. To sit on his lap with my thin nightgown on. I didn't want to, but she made me. *Why didn't she protect me? I was a child!!* The child she claimed she loved and wanted. She aided in the abuse and prostituted me. *Did she hate me that much?? What did I do to deserve this treatment from her?*

Being inappropriately touched all those years caused my sexual nature to arise, and I began acting out. While I was not experiencing actual intercourse, by nine years old, I was engaged in touching, grinding, and other mild foreplay. I had been exposed to it, and since they kept coming back, I must have been good at something. So, instead of being a victim and being forced to go along with whoever Addie brought in, I decided to choose who I wanted to touch me. That seems twisted as I write the words, but that was my frame of mind. In a weird way, I was taking my power and control back. If I got to choose, then I wouldn't feel as awful or dirty about the act. This was the beginning of a dark path.

> *Have you ever felt unprotected and all alone? This one was a hard pill for me to swallow and face. First, acknowledging that I had been molested and then admitting that set my course of an unhealthy sexual nature. Have you ever been violated? Have you ever been taken advantage of? Have you ever been put in situations where you have felt awkward and ashamed of what happened or how it made you feel? First, you are not alone, and it was not your fault. Even if it was a bad choice leading up to it, it was still not your fault. No is no, and anything done against your will and without your permission is a violation to you. No one has a right to touch you or place you in a position that is sexual in nature or leaves you powerless.*
>
> *This next reflection may be a bit more difficult, but you got this. Take a deep breath and then begin.*

Unprotected- Reflection

> *He who dwells in the shelter of the Most High will remain secure and rest in the shadow of the Almighty [whose power no enemy can withstand]. I will say of the Lord, "He is my refuge and my fortress, My God, in whom I trust [with great confidence, and on whom I rely]!" For He will save you from the trap of the fowler, And from the deadly pestilence. He will cover you and completely protect you with His pinions, And under His wings you will find refuge; His faithfulness is a shield and a wall. You will not be afraid of the terror of night, Nor of the arrow that flies by day, - Psalms 91:1-5 (AMP)*

This time, during your reflection, sit and think about a time (and it could be more than one) when you felt violated, you were violated, or your choice was taken from you in a situation, and you felt powerless. Face the pain. Deal with the hurt. You cannot heal and move forward until you face the past and gather your broken pieces. As the pain resurfaces, you may need to seek counseling help to move past it. This will not be a simple journal of my feelings, and I am done. You will have to dig deep. And what you may find in the digging you may not like or be ready for. But once you start, don't give up. There is healing on the other side. Are you ready? Deep breaths. Allow the tears to fall as you release all you have felt concerning this moment and what you are about to uncover.

Breathe! It's okay; you are not there anymore, and they can no longer hurt you. Deep breaths. Allow the tears to flow. Tears are healing and liquid prayers to God. Don't shut them off. Begin to write what you wanted to say but were not allowed to say. Scream it! Shout it! Yell it! Whatever you need to do, get it out. You have a voice—no more suffering in silence.

Breathe! Get help so that you can heal. This was a heavy one. Get the help you need to truly heal from this trauma. You may have to do it in steps and segments. But don't stop; keep moving; you can do this.

Chapter 6

Why Me?

Sitting in the lonely, cold room, I could hardly keep up with all of the toxic thoughts rushing through my mind. As I sat on the bed shaking and pulling at my hair, I tried to find the strength to do anything except SCREAM, but I couldn't. The thoughts were overwhelming and consumed me until all I could do was shout, "You are so weak, you are worthless, you are ruined!!!"

I began yelling at myself in the same old, wooden, and termite-damaged mirror more and more. I was back in the room on the bed in front of the mirror. I looked down at the prescription bottle in my trembling hands. I had a vice grip on the bottle and a couple of muscle relaxers in my other hand. My tears had stained my pink and blue shirt and were splashing down on my jeans.

Why didn't my parents love me? Why didn't they protect me? Racing thoughts came from every angle, rushing over me like violent tsunami waves. I screamed at God with every ounce of energy I could muster, "WHY ME? WHY DID YOU ALLOW THIS TO HAPPEN TO ME, GOD? The ones who should have loved me didn't, and the one person who did, you took away from me. I want answers, God. I need to know."

As I continued to sob uncontrollably, I knew so many of the tears were because I still wanted to be loved. No More! I couldn't trust love would come for me. So, I decided I didn't want to do this living thing anymore. My life was too much for one person to bear. *How could you allow them to hurt me this way? I was a child, and I should have been protected. But you say that you love everyone. Well, You can't love me because if You did, then You would not have allowed this to happen to me. You would have given me parents who loved me and protected me. Ones that would be there for me. But You did not. Why? Why, God, did you abandon me also?* My emotions were like an uncontrollable bouncy ball. I was yelling at Addie, I was yelling at this figment of myself in the mirror, and I was yelling at God—a pill popped here, a sip of gin and juice there. This party to end all others was in progress. *No one cares about me, not even God.* So, who was going to stop me?

During my lifetime, I thought at least God cared. That's what I was taught at church. Looking over my life and remembering all the hurt and pain that I had endured, He couldn't have cared. "For God so loved the world, that he gave his only begotten Son, that whosoever believeth in him should not perish, but have everlasting life" (John 3:16 KJV). *Well, God, am I not a part of the world? Therefore, You should love me.* Just one more lie that had been told to me. I stared at the pills that seemed to have multiplied in my hand. Is this what I had been reduced to? Pain so excruciating it felt like someone was doing open-heart surgery on me while

I was awake. Wanting me to feel every ounce of pain with each cut. I just wanted to be numb to it all; then maybe, just maybe, it wouldn't hurt so much. *Why Me? God, why did You leave me when I needed you the most?*

> *As you think back over your life, even up until now, have you ever felt that God abandoned you? Do you even believe in God? Some people can't believe in someone they have never seen. As you begin reflecting here, who were (or are) you mad at when it comes to how your life has turned out? Who did you yell at when all the pain and hurt came crashing down?*

Abandoned and Alone - Reflection

Have you ever read the poem "Footprints in the Sand? While the original author of it remains unclear, the poem tells the story of someone walking through their relationship with Jesus. The person in the poem finds themselves in a horribly difficult time in life. A time so devastating they feel like The Lord abandoned them. In a moment of talking with God, the person inquires where He had been through the hard days. The Lord has the person look back at the sand on the beach, and He tells them those places where they only see one set of footprints is during the seasons He carried them.

My life reminds me of this poem. When I looked at my life through flashing scenes, where I was at the very lowest and saddest times, there was only one set of footprints. But I knew before that there were two. I felt like God didn't understand when I needed Him the most, so He left me. But He never did. The Lord responded that, during those times when I could only see that one set of footprints, He was carrying me. That was still hard for me to believe at first. But I'm glad I know it now.

Have you ever been so hurt and mad that you began to yell at God? I mean, really scream at God and maybe even cuss at Him because you are so hurt and angry. Well, I have been there. How could a loving and sovereign God allow all the pain and suffering in my life? That was my mindset, and I am sure you can attest to a moment (or moments) in your life where you have had that sentiment toward God. Does that make you a bad person? No, it makes us human, and we are still His children.

Growing up, we were taught not to question our parents because that was disrespectful. But God is our Father, and He wants us to come to Him, even when we are angry. It is in those times of conversation that He reveals that He is still with us and has never left us. He will help us through it: all the good, the bad, the ugly, and the worst. God never promised us an easy, pain-free life. He promised that He would be with us every step of the way.

> *"The LORD himself goes before you and will be with you; he will never leave you nor forsake you. Do not be afraid; do not be discouraged." Deuteronomy 31:8 (NIV)*

At what moment in your life have you been angry with God and felt as though He had left you? Write it down. Be honest. Only in honesty can you truly heal. No one is judging you.

Now, go back and reread Deuteronomy 31:8. With a change of perspective, you can see where God was still there in the midst of the pain and kept you. How does that change your viewpoint now if it does?

Chapter 7

I Need Love

I'm desperate; I need love! I had become sexually active around 13 going on 14 years of age. Being molested and pimped out at an early age, I realized, far too young, that I had something men wanted. I decided to see if they, in return, had something that I wanted. Instead of feeling disgusted by what was done to me, how could I turn this in my favor?

Sex is what made me feel loved. The close connection to that person, being wrapped in their embrace and feeling safe, loved, desired, and wanted for a moment. Since I didn't have at least untainted love growing up, sexual moments filled the voids that I had within me. Thinking back, I had love here and there, but it was often interrupted or watered down. I wanted a love that was consistent and without conditions of doing this or doing that so I would act as if I love you.

With sex, I got to hear those three little words that meant so much, "I love you!" I was able to feel desired and wanted, even if it was for a short period of time. I later discovered that the words were more caught up in the moment than an actual expression of what love is. But I loved the feeling the lie gave me, and I lived it as much as possible because I needed it in my life.

Being abandoned by both parents, losing my grandfather, and not feeling wanted or loved as a child, only in spurts - if that. I wanted and craved to be loved by someone, anyone. I saw those around me being nurtured and loved, and I saw it on television. But that was the problem. I saw it for others and didn't see it, feel it, or have it for myself. So, if having sex gave me the feeling of being loved that I needed and craved, then sex it was.

My mommy was back in my life and had been with us since before my granddaddy Ves died. Even though she was present, the love I wanted and needed from her was not fulfilled.

Our relationship was strained because of Addie's interference. We struggled to find balance and harmony as mother and daughter. My mommy didn't leave as she had before. She chose to stay present in my life despite her mother's opposition.

Due to time apart, the little time we spent together, and tension, our relationship faced many hill and valley moments. My mommy was still searching for real love herself and, in her own way, gave me the love that she knew how to give.

She was dating different men looking to fill her own loveless voids. Because she was trying to fill her own holes, she didn't see mine. She didn't realize that my deep, dark holes of emptiness mirrored her own. At that time, I didn't understand it. All I saw was broken promises from the time she came back. She would make plans and cancel them at the last minute or bring one of her friends with us. Most of the time, she canceled them to go out with one of her male friends. She had time for everyone else but me, her only daughter. The only child Addie allowed her to keep. You see, my mother had gotten pregnant again after me, but Addie refused to raise another child, so she made my mother give him up for adoption. So, I was not vying for my mommy's attention from another sibling but from other people in her life. She was back but still absent.

During those years of trying to rebuild my relationship with my mommy, I became a mother myself. For some reason, I believed that by having a child, I would have the love that I longed to experience. I figured if I loved my own baby, it would simply love me back. Problem solved, or so I thought. I was 16 years old, going on 17 the following month when my first son was born. *What did I know about being a mother?* My mother had me when she was 15 because she didn't know real love either. A repeated cycle.

My mommy was so angry with me when she found out I was pregnant. This was the last thing she wanted or needed in her life. She stopped talking to me for almost three months. The silence was horrific. I was emotional and had questions, but she would barely say two words to me. The look of disdain in her eyes when she saw me was painful. I needed my mother's love and touch, but all I got was her cold shoulder. Some days, the pain was too great to bear.

I was young and pregnant. My body was going through changes, as well as my emotions. I needed someone to talk to. Not just someone but my mommy. Yes, Addie was there, but she kept the fuel of silence going between my mommy and me. It felt like she delighted in our pain of not speaking to one another. I would sometimes muster the courage to ask my mommy a question, and she would either shake her head at me or give an extremely short, cold answer. Many times, I sat alone in my room in tears. Crying not only because I became pregnant early and was unsure how I was going to be a parent but because I needed my mommy. She was there physically, but emotionally and mentally, she was absent.

Eventually, my mommy came around; it turned out she was more hurt than angry. "I never wanted you to experience what I did when I became pregnant at a young age. I just didn't know how to say that to you," she explained. Those were her first real words to me in months. She explained to me how hard it was being a young mother. I would miss out on many things and be restricted in where I could go. Because if the baby couldn't go, then I couldn't go.

We both cried and hugged for a long time. Oh, to feel her touch and love again was priceless. Our love language was physical touch. We would hug often, kiss one another, and tell each other how much we loved each other. During the time when we were not speaking, none of those things happened. It was as if I was in an emotional drought. Hearing her speak to me directly and more than just a short cold phrase was music to my ears. As she cradled me in her arms, I felt such love and warmth. It was the feeling of being wrapped in a warm, cozy blanket on a cold day.

"Thank you, Mommy, for talking to me again, and I'm so sorry that I disappointed you," I sobbed. My tears became a mixture of relief that she was talking to me, understanding why she stopped talking to me, sadness that I disappointed her, and joy that she was fully interacting with me again.

"It's okay. We will get through this together," she replied. We continued to embrace each other. Was this real? I prayed it was real and not a dream; if so, I didn't want to wake up. It was real for the first time in a long time. We sat and talked. As we talked, I began to understand why she had been so upset with me about getting pregnant early.

She never wanted me to go through all of what she experienced as a teen, becoming pregnant too soon. The one thing my mommy was clear on was that when I had this baby, he was my baby and my responsibility. She would help when she could, but she was not taking over or taking custody like Addie did with her.

Then, the second part of the cycle was initiated. The grandmother wanted to take my son and raise him for me because I was a child and knew nothing about raising one. She made comments here and there when I was pregnant. After he was born, she always came to our side of the house to see if I was doing this or that right. At first, she offered to take him and allow me to live my life. A couple of months later, she became more insistent on raising him.

I protested because I wanted his love all for me, and I had experienced firsthand what it was like to be torn from your mother. The other thing that stood in Addie's way was my son's other grandparents. They and Addie were in a power struggle. They made sure that he got everything he needed and that they got the time they wanted with him, not the amount of time Addie wanted to allow. He was their first grandchild, and they demanded bi-weekly visits.

The struggle between Addie and my son's paternal grandparents would get intense at times. Addie was used to telling people what to do, and they did it. If not, she would yell, cuss, and fuss, and then they would usually back down and give in. Not them. They wanted and deserved time with their grandson. They helped with many of his necessities and helped me by doing so. They would not be moved by Addie's behavior.

Of course, Addie made every attempt to poison my relationship with them so that she could get her way.

"You know his people used you for their son's pleasure. Now you are stuck with a baby, and he is living the life," she would say repeatedly.

"No, they didn't." I would push back. "He loves me. He would not hurt me!" We were young, and I thought that we were in love. We had even talked about marriage, and I believed him, so I knew that Addie's words were manipulation.

"You so stupid! No man loves you. Men just want what you are giving away, and then they're on to the next. All men are dogs; you just have to know how to train them," Addie stated.

What? *"All men are dogs, and you have to know how to train them." So, the ones coming back and forth to see you, are they trained, or are you?"* I would dare not say aloud what I was thinking.

As much as I rejected Addie's words about my son's father, he did end up breaking my heart. But I was not giving that old lady the satisfaction of saying, "I told you so, so." For about a month, I hid the fact that we were no longer together. The tragic reality was I did catch him cheating on me with another girl at a pool. I was supposed to be in the house as part of my six-week post-delivery recovery. I wanted to go for a ride and get out of the house. It had been four weeks by then, and I finally convinced my mommy and Addie to allow me to go for a ride with my friend, LaShawn. Of course, we chose to go see our boyfriends.

Well, they were not home, but they were together. After learning they had gone swimming at an apartment building, my boyfriend's younger brother, LaShawn, and I went to look for them. We grabbed Slurpees® before heading there. As we walked toward the pool, we saw people laughing and playing. But we were only looking for the two who belonged to us. His little brother stopped, but I kept going. At the time, I didn't realize that he had spotted him first. There he was, hugged up on another girl. She had her legs wrapped around his waist in the pool. She kissed him, and then they went under the water. A friend of his was trying to get his attention, but it was too late. When he came up out of the water, I swung on him. That startled him and the girl. Once he cleared the water from his eyes and gathered his thoughts, he realized it was me. His eyes widened in disbelief. I began yelling, screaming, cursing, and crying. I snatched the necklace he gave me off my neck and threw it at him. The girl said something slick, and I started in on her-yelling, screaming, and cursing her out.

I was just about to jump in the pool because I was so angry when his friend and LaShawn grabbed me. They both yelled. "No, you just had a baby."

I didn't care at that moment. I was pissed and hurt. His little brother grabbed me, hugged me, and said, "It's going to be okay. Let's go." The sound of his voice was so sweet and caring. He helped to soothe the agonizing pain moving through me.

When Addie finally found out we were not together, she couldn't wait to gloat. "You stupid, and you are hardheaded. I told you that boy didn't care about you. Now he found him a better girl to be with, and you still stuck with a baby!"

With courage that came out of nowhere, I stood up for myself, "He may have left me, but I still love my son, and I am going to take care of him whether he helps or not." I didn't wait for her to respond. I headed to my room, held him, looked at him, and asked, "You love me, don't you? And you always will because I will always love you."

He was almost two months old, but he cooed at me with a sweet smile, and I kissed his little cheek. From that moment, I put all my life into my son. His paternal grandparents didn't stop helping or taking him for visits. They were upset about how things happened, but that was our relationship. That had no bearing on the relationship with their grandson.

My second son was conceived in my last year of high school. I missed everything - homecoming, prom, Grad Nite, senior skip day, but I never resented my son. I didn't blame him at all; it was because of my choices and actions. I already had one child, and now here was number two. The painful truth is that I was not sure who the father was. I was still messing with my firstborn's dad and would be with another guy when we were arguing. Even though we had broken up, I still loved him deeply. I had hoped that we could work things out and become a family. We did have a child together, after all. I felt certain and prayed that the boys had the same father. Although I was torn about what to do concerning this pregnancy (and Addie's comments didn't help any), I chose to keep my son. I was nervous about telling my mommy that I was pregnant again. She was living in her own place and had gotten married again. She was not happy, but she was still there for me. Once again, she made sure I knew that this was my baby and I had to be responsible for both children. She would help when she could or wanted to.

It was not his fault that his mother was all over the place and broken. I would love him because he was my son. When he was born, he had a hole in his heart and some initial breathing issues. I was so scared. Anxious thoughts flooded my mind. *Had I cursed him because of the things that I had said while I was pregnant? Had Addie cursed him because of the things she said?* All I could do was cry and pray that my baby would be okay. I never knew how much I loved him until I almost lost him. He was having trouble breathing on his own. They kept doing CPR and had to place him on a breathing machine. I wanted to hold my son, but I couldn't. The doctors had to make sure that he was stable first. My mommy was there with me, holding my hand as I prayed.

"God, please let him be okay. I'm sorry for my mistakes. Please don't take it out on him. Please let him live, I love him."

Hours later, I was finally able to hold him and love on him. We did have many doctor appointments during his first year of life. But thank God, by the time he was around two years old, the hole in his heart began to close, and he didn't need surgery.

By then, I was the mother to two sons, two men in my life who, if I loved hard enough, wouldn't leave me. Or so I thought. To my disappointment, the love I sought was still missing. There was a huge hole in my heart, and no matter how hard I tried it continued to expand. Going from relationship to relationship and looking to my children, who were just babies themselves, to fill me didn't work. Why would I continue to seek love from men who couldn't love me? Was there a method to my madness for love? Maybe. I liked my men tall, handsome, with pretty eyes. Initially, I went for the light-skinned guys, but then I started to fall for the chocolate ones. I later realized that I had a daddy complex (he wasn't there). My dad was a chocolate man, so by going out with light-skinned guys, I thought, well, they would love me; they would want me because the chocolate man (my dad) didn't. I was shown that love was bought or could be bought. In my desperation, I would do extra stuff for them, like buying gifts to keep them interested in me. This was so I could get what I thought was love.

The grandmother said, "You are stupid; you should be getting paid to sleep with them, not just giving it away."

My response was, "Well, if I did that, then that would make me a whore, and I am not that."

She laughed, "You are a whore, just a broke one," then walked away.

Anger burned within me. Why would she call me a whore? She was the whore, not me. I didn't see myself as a whore. A whore used men for money and what they could get. I genuinely wanted love.

Looking back, I was using them more than they were using me. Had I become a pimp unknowingly? I considered myself the shot caller; I paid them for what I wanted. I was in charge; no one was taking anything from me anymore.

Well, it was only a service, and that was the feeling of love. For me, it was not about sex; it was about feeling loved. The sex was just the vehicle that got me what I wanted. Thinking more about it, I guess I was a whore. I was sleeping with them to get a feeling I desired: love, not money. I had become what Addie said. I had become a love whore. But I was a good whore. I could get who I wanted and how often I wanted them. When you know how to use what you got, then you can get what you want.

> *Have you ever been so desperate for love that you would do anything? Yeah, you might talk a good game in front of people, but behind closed doors, no one really knows what is going on. As you begin this reflection section, think about those things that you have done for love, or to fill the void of love.*

Looking for Love in All the Wrong Places-Reflections

If I could speak all the languages of earth and of angels, but didn't love others, I would only be a noisy gong or a clanging cymbal. If I had the gift of prophecy, and if I understood all of God's secret plans and possessed all knowledge, and if I had such faith that I could move mountains, but didn't love others, I would be nothing. If I gave everything I have to the poor and even sacrificed my body, I could boast about it; but if I didn't love others, I would have gained nothing.

Love is patient and kind. Love is not jealous or boastful or proud or rude. It does not demand its own way. It is not irritable, and it keeps no record of being wronged. It does not rejoice about injustice but rejoices whenever the truth wins out. Love never gives up, never loses faith, is always hopeful, and endures through every circumstance.

Prophecy and speaking in unknown languages and special knowledge will become useless. But love will last forever! Now our knowledge is partial and incomplete, and even the gift of prophecy reveals only part of the whole picture! But when the time of perfection comes, these partial things will become useless.

When I was a child, I spoke and thought and reasoned as a child. But when I grew up, I put away childish things. Now we see things imperfectly, like puzzling reflections in a mirror, but then we will see everything with perfect clarity. All that I know now is partial

> *and incomplete, but then I will know everything completely, just as God now knows me completely.*
>
> *Three things will last forever—faith, hope, and love—and the greatest of these is love.*
>
> *1 Corinthians 13:1-13 (NLT)*

Wanting to be loved and needing to be loved are different. A want is something that you can live with or without. It's something that would be nice to have, but you can get by without it. But a need - a need is essential for your life. And without certain essentials, you can die.

Without love, you can die in an emotional and spiritual sense. Some people have said and even equated the lack of love with a natural death by saying they died of a broken heart. The lack of love can be detrimental to one's health and livelihood. Love is an intense, deep affection for another person. Love is many things. Even when psychologist Abraham Maslow developed his hierarchy of needs, he included "Love" on the list. It begins with **physiological** (food and clothing), **safety** (job security), **love and belonging needs** (friendship), **esteem**, and **self-actualization**. These are the basic needs that every person desires and are necessary for their life.

To be deprived of real love can leave you broken, hopeless, and feeling as if you have died or are about to die. Now is a good time for deep introspection. What does your love meter look like? How much love are you giving out? Better question: how much love are you taking in? If you are not receiving as much or more of what you are putting out, there could be a deficiency. In the deficiency, we tend to make not-so-good choices to get what we feel we lack.

What are you doing to get love or the sense of love in your life?

Do you love you? Seems like an easy question, right? But do you love yourself if you put yourself in compromising situations to receive love or a sense of love? Do you love yourself enough to hold on to your values and make others respect those values and you, so that you can be loved properly? Think about it. Do you love yourself enough, even if it means being alone?

Chapter 8

Blindsided- By a Ton of Bricks (Trigger Warning)

What the what? How did this happen? While looking for love in definitely all the wrong places, I continued making bad choices with guys. One of those bad choices landed me in an abusive relationship. For the purpose of this story, we will call him MX. It didn't start off abusive, nor were there any signs that he was violent. He honestly appeared as a knight in shining armor and then later turned into Dr. Jekyll and Mr. Hyde - nice and sweet one minute, then angry and mad the next.

He was helpful and attentive at first. He would help me around the house, pick up a few things that he saw that I needed, and interact with my sons. He even made me believe he wanted me to be a better person. He would say cursing didn't look good on me and ladies should not use such words. He didn't see me as an object but as a lady. This was significant due to everything I had gone through growing up. MX made me feel special. He told me what I longed to hear: he loved me, wanted to be with me, and would protect me. He basically told me everything I had told him I was missing, but in his own words.

It turns out he just wanted me to be another person, someone he had loved and lost; I was the surrogate to his missing piece, I would later realize. I was just a replacement for the one he said he wanted to be with. His care and concern for me to be a better person seemed genuine. My mother saw through it, but I didn't. MX would correct me on how I spoke, how I dressed, what I watched, and even the music I listened to. It all happened subtly.

How did I miss the signs? Was I that desperate, or was I so intrigued by his appearance? I mean, MX was tall, dark, and seemed handsome enough to me at the time. He had nice brown eyes, but not like the ones I had fallen head over heels for before, although they were nice enough. He was of a lean-to-medium build, not too shabby to look at. And let me tell you something: his smile pulled you in. MX went to church regularly and rarely used any cuss words, which was foreign to me. Because Addie could cuss up a storm and would cuss, I also picked that up.

In the beginning, it was a nice change, feeling loved and respected. Having someone in my life who believed I could be a better person. Things were put in place subtly. Control doesn't happen overnight; you have to cleverly ease it in with the most loving and concerned ways, so the person doesn't suspect it. Control happens when a person manipulates the important and endearing things to you. He was no different. He would say things like he was worried about me, so I needed to call him when I left home and got to my destination. When Mommy found out about this, she didn't like it. She thought he was being controlling toward me. She kept preaching to me that no one person should have that much control over you. Mesmerized by his love, I dismissed her concerns. I sure did because he loved me, right? Little did I know that Mommy was speaking from wisdom and experience at the time because she had gone through this in one of her prior marriages. So, she recognized all the signs and red flags, like how MX would cut up if I forgot to check in on time. When I missed check-in or didn't reach my check-in point by the time I said I would, he would get angry and yell at me.

Then, after he would tell me off, MX would say lines like, "I only got angry with you because I was worried about you and had no way of checking to make sure that you were alright."

Even though I did not like the delivery, his answer felt sincere. It had to be because he loved me, right? And these were those warning signs my mommy spoke of that I didn't see because I was dazzled by the light of love - false love.

As the months passed, which soon turned into years, MX's demeanor gradually changed. His aggression increased; he began cussing and became physical. He started hitting me, choking me, and twisting my arm. How did I get here? This was not supposed to happen to me again. I didn't want this abuse, but I didn't want to be alone. Addie always said, "A piece of man is better than no man at all," which was her motto. I hated hearing that back then but was beginning to live it.

You see, through the years MX and I were together, there was cheating (known and unknown). Even still, it was too hard to walk away. After everything this man put me through, people thought I was crazy to still be with him. I had been deceived. I was blinded by the pretty web of lies and flattery. The web had been spun, trapping me as its prey. As each month and year passed, the web that was spun placed me tighter and tighter into its web of deception with MX.

I had no clue that I was under attack mentally and emotionally; those abuses were designed to wear me down to be attacked physically. The allusion of his love controlled my mind; I was trapped in the web of all his deception. An intricately designed web to lure me in, get me caught up, and remain trapped for what felt like an eternity. I felt stuck with no way out. Have you ever felt trapped and wanted to leave, but in every direction you looked, there was no exit, doors, or windows? That is what this relationship felt like. I was stuck in a sticky situation with no way to escape. It was as though no one cared about what I was going through or cared to hear my cries for help. The one person who did see it early on was my mother, but I didn't listen to her warning. Once she died, things seemed to get worse between me and MX. Why didn't I listen to her?

The demonic attacks around me amped up. At this point in my life, I wanted to become more a part of the church. I no longer desired to be a "hoe," yet still, the demonic activity around me grew increasingly worse. I do not want to spook anyone out, but some nights, I would wake up pinned to the bed, yet no one was there. Imagine opening your eyes to get out of bed and being unable to move. Like there is a heavy two-ton weight lying on you, and you are powerless. You try to open your mouth to scream, but nothing comes. You're struggling to breathe. You look around and see everything in your room, so you know it's not a dream. Yet, you can't move. The more you try, it's a struggle; every part of your body is weighted down. That's what those moments felt like to me.

It would get so bad that, at times, I was dragged from my bed onto the floor and almost under my bed. There was no one or nothing there. But yet, there was this dark presence that I couldn't see but could feel. The darkness came to life; it was a demon. No red horns or long tails like in the movies, just pure blackness.

I can recall coming home from church one day; I was telling MX all about the demonic attacks that I had been having and how I was scared to go to sleep at home. As we continued talking about it, we pulled up in front of my house, and as I looked up at my window, I saw it. It was the middle of the day, the sun was shining bright, and no clouds in the sky. Yet I saw a demon in my window staring at me. It was blacker than black but still very visible. It had no eyes per se, yet you could still see the coldness where the eyes would be. I was horrified to my core. It was waiting for me to come into the house. I asked him if he saw it, and he acted as if he did not. *Was this a part of the game to keep me bound and close to him? Was I losing my mind? What the Hello Kitty® was going on?* He brushed it off as nothing, but I still had to go into that house where it was waiting for me. I gathered myself and went inside. What else was I to do? It was my home.

By mid-1995, I became pregnant again. Since MX's demeanor had changed, I was nervous about telling him. We had already gone through many changes and infidelity on his part by that point. Initially, I thought I had a stomach bug or maybe the flu. I had been getting sick at work and vomiting. So, I went to the doctor since it was not getting any better. Then I found out that I was pregnant. I went back and forth in my mind on how and when to tell him. When I finally did tell him, he exploded, as I feared. Do you remember in the cartoons when the person would get so fiery red their whole head would swell up and then explode all over the place? Yes, the news garnered that kind of explosion. He began yelling, cussing, and throwing things. Not the response that I had desired. I was called every name under the sun but a child of God. He almost sounded like Addie. Well, he was definitely not "Team New Baby." He blamed me for not being more responsible in ensuring that a pregnancy didn't happen.

I had not told my mommy or anyone else yet. MX was so angry. I felt alone and scared. This made baby number three! The aftermath of telling him left me heartbroken. I didn't want to go through that again with my mother and Addie. But a few days after being accused of being sexually irresponsible by MX, I finally mustered up the courage to tell my mother and Addie. Although Mommy was disappointed, she was there for me; she was my rock. We talked through this one - unlike the first time when we didn't speak for months. She asked how it happened, how he reacted, and what he would do. I told her what happened, his reaction, and he didn't want me to have the baby, but I was keeping my baby. She was not happy at all with how he treated me when he found out. She said she would help when she could, but again, this child was my responsibility, and it didn't look like I would get much help from him. She held me and allowed me to cry and be comforted in her arms.

Addie, on the other hand, could not stop talking, "You are so dumb and stupid. How did you allow that to happen?"

How did I get into this predicament once again? Addie even accused me of trying to trap him into staying with me by getting pregnant again. That was definitely not the case. I was on birth control pills, but they didn't work. I had gotten sick and was given an antibiotic. I did not know that while on that, it changes the effect of the birth control pills. My hands were already full with my two sons. MX was clear he wasn't interested in being or ready to be an actual parent, and as time passed, he clearly had no intentions of filling the role of stepparent. Although he knew being with me meant there were already two children involved with whatever relationship would be.

I had conceived, and before you knew it, she would be here, and she was staying. Despite what anyone said, I was not aborting my child or giving her up for adoption. Yes, it was a girl, a precious baby girl. For most of my pregnancy, I had to keep it a secret from MX's family. He was unhappy and said his family would react worse than he did once they found out. He tried several times to convince me to abort my baby, but I refused. I had made my bed and would lie in it, as the old folks would say. How could I take a life that God had blessed me with? When the news finally came out to his family, it was not as bad as I was led to believe. I had to tell them as he was not going to do it. I was tense and nervous because of everything he had told me about how they would react. Once I told them, I was waiting for them to explode like MX had. They were unhappy about it but were not mean or nasty either. They shared how they felt and asked how I planned to care for her. They advised that they would be supportive and help since it was their grandchild.

After seeing their reaction, MX began to grasp that we were having a baby. He took me to the hospital when it was time for me to deliver, and he was in the delivery room when she came. After she was born, his parents came to the hospital to visit her. They were excited to meet their first grandchild. My mommy came to the hospital as well to check on me and her. Addie waited until I came home to see her. MX came to spend time with her. When I went back to work, his mom kept the baby girl so she didn't have to go to daycare. Mommy spent time with her, too, when she was able.

During the first year of baby girl's life, my mommy became sick, and I was helping to take care of her alongside my bonus daddy. Over time, she had gotten so weak that she could not be home alone while he went to work. Mom had been diagnosed with a rare disease called scleroderma, which was affecting her internal organs and her body. I would take her to many of her doctor's appointments and fight on her behalf with the insurance company to get the supplies she needed. During this time, I had moved out of Addie's house and had my own apartment with my three children. I had to go back to work, so I could not always be at her home. My mom and daddy had to move in with Addie, so there would always be someone with her.

I felt like Mommy's sickness came at such an inconvenient time. We had just begun to repair our relationship from all the drama, pain, and lies that Addie had told us both. This time, after previous attempts by Addie to keep us separated, I finally had my mommy back and the relationship I desired with her. It was hard seeing her sick and not as vibrant as she used to be. Mommy was medium height and had a nice figure. She had caramel-colored skin like me and had brownish hair. Her smile was warm and heavenly. Her love and laughter were like the perfect sweater that made you feel good when you wore it. Knowing what she looked like before and how she looked by then was hard for me. Her features were changing before my eyes, and at times, it was hard for me to go to her house and help take care of her. She used to be so strong and lively. I wanted my daughter to experience all the love and fun that she had to offer. Trips to the park, movie nights, bedtime stories, and more, but she wouldn't. I was hurt and angry with God. *Why was He doing this to my mommy?* She was a good person, unlike Addie.

Even though it was hard to see her like that, at the end of the day, I would be there for my mommy. I would go and help care for her after work when I could. It was rough some days. I had my baby girl, who wasn't one yet, and two boys running around. Some days would be full. I would have to go to the store and get her certain things to eat and drink. Due to the illness, she couldn't eat regular foods, so I had to go to the health food store across town. Some days, I would fix her meals if Daddy Thee (Theodis) couldn't. Her meals had to be prepared in a specific way, so she didn't get sick. She was on an oxygen machine, and I was the only one she wanted to clean it. I knew how to do it according to the doctor's instructions, so she didn't get sick afterward. Cleaning it had to be done weekly.

Besides doing those things for my mommy, my sons were in school, so that meant homework most nights, and with an infant in tow, there were diaper changes and then potty training. Not to mention, I had to be at MX's beck and call. But she was my mother, and I would do whatever she needed me to do. I loved her dearly. I will not lie and say it was easy because it wasn't. I was a new mother again, this time to a little girl, so it was like learning motherhood all over again while caring for my mother. I had to be strong for her. Whereas before I could lean on her, she now needed to lean on me. Many nights, I cried myself to sleep because I felt overwhelmed by everything.

June, the year after my mommy got sick, Mommy and her husband, Daddy Thee, bought me a cake and a birthday card. So, I went to see her and pick up my gifts. She wanted me to cut the cake so that she could share a slice with me. This was a huge request because eating even a piece of the cake could make her feel worse. I was so brainwashed at the time by the relationship with MX that I told her I wanted him to see it first, take a picture of it, and then I would bring her a piece back. She looked so sad and disappointed, but she replied, "Okay."

I remember hurrying back home to show him the cake they had gotten me, but he was not there. So, I called him to see where he was. Come to find out, he chose to go hang out at a friend's house. It was my birthday, but he said, "He and his wife invited me over for dinner. I will come after." I was crushed. I disappointed my mommy by choosing to rush home to spend time and celebrate with him, and he was somewhere else, somewhere I was not invited to.

I sat at home alone, looking at the cake, waiting and wishing I would have stayed with my mommy and Daddy Thee and celebrated with them. I rushed home, thinking he would be there to spend time with him. The kids went to their grandparents' house. So, I just sat there in an empty house, staring at the cake. I left a house where my parents wanted to celebrate and honor me to go home and be alone and disappointed. It was my birthday, and MX was spending time with other people and not me. This was a new pain that I was feeling. I had inflicted this onto myself because of my choices.

When he finally showed up hours later, he barely looked at the cake and definitely didn't want any. Crushed and disappointed all over again, I decided to wait and cut the cake with my mommy as she had originally requested. I would bring her to my house on my next day off, and it would be our special time. I called her and told her I was picking her up early on Thursday so she could come over and spend the day with me.

Her response was, “We will see.” I thought she was saying that because she thought I would change my mind because of him, but that was not why she kept responding to me that way.

That Wednesday, my mother paged me to call her. I was at work, so I called her on my break. When I called her, she began apologizing for different things that had happened over the years. I said, “It’s okay, Mommy, don’t worry about it.”

But she insisted, “No, Tina, I need to hear you say that you forgive me.”

I kept saying, “Mommy, it is okay.” She would not relent until I said it. Because I had to get back to work, I finally obliged her and said, “Mommy, I forgive you, and I love you.”

She breathed in such a way that I paid close attention to her. I could see the relief in her eyes as she said, “Thank you, sweetheart. That is what I needed to hear. You are still coming by the house before you go home, right?” Before getting off the phone, I told her I was still coming by when I got off work, and we would still spend the next day together, and once again, she responded, “We will see.”

When I finished my shift, I stopped by the house to check on her and my second son, who was there with them for the week, before I went to pick up my baby girl. Mommy was on the porch in her chair, getting some fresh air. She was breathing scattered. I asked her if I needed to clean her oxygen machine or do anything before I went home. She just smiled at me and said, “No.” I didn’t stay that long because I planned to have her all to myself the next day, and Addie kept coming over to that side of the house to disturb our conversation. I kissed my mommy goodbye and said I would see her tomorrow, only to get the same response, “We will see.”

My feelings were hurt. *Had I disappointed my mother so much that she did not believe that I would come and pick her up?* I was determined to prove her wrong and make her proud of me again so she didn't have to second guess what I told her. Baby girl was at her other grandma's house and staying a bit longer because they had family coming in from out of town, and they wanted to see her. I went home to rest and prepare for my mommy's visit the next day. So much had been going on since Mommy had gotten sick. We had not had any alone time just to sit, talk, and love on one another without interruptions. I wanted time alone with her; I needed it. To be able to sit at home alone was a nice change from all the running around I had been doing the past few months. Peace and quiet embraced me for the moment.

> *I was so caught up in the relationship that I ignored the warnings and the signs. It appeared at first as real love, but it wasn't. I didn't see the forest for the trees. As you reflect on this chapter, I know it was a lot. Take a moment and gather yourself before moving into this time of reflection.*

Out of Nowhere Reflections

> *The Lord is close to the brokenhearted and saves those who are crushed in spirit. - Psalm 34:18 (NIV)*

Have you expected things to go a certain way? You plan perfectly and meticulously, and then it all goes wrong out of nowhere. The person seems perfect, maybe too perfect, but you are so caught up that you don't see, or you ignore, all the red flags. It has happened to many of us. Think of a time when you were blindsided or caught off guard by a situation, leaving you in a tailspin. Did you recover? Are you still trying to recover?

Have you forgiven yourself for walking into the situation even though the warnings were there? Have you forgiven the person or persons? Or are you still holding on to the offenses and keeping a tally of how and when they hurt you? Release it and forgive them, not for them but for you. Forgiveness frees you, your mind, and your body from future pain.

> *For if I forgive others their trespasses [their reckless and willful sins, leaving them, letting them go, and giving up resentment], my heavenly Father will also forgive you. - Matthew 6:14 AMP*

Chapter 9

The Call (Trigger Warning)

Have you ever had a moment in time that you will never forget? I have had many, but one call created a moment for me that would impact the rest of my life. Daddy Thee called me, fussing about not seeing Mommy that day. I told him that I had been there a few hours ago, and we talked about me picking her up the next day. As we spoke, I could hear my mommy faintly in the background, telling him I stopped by, and we talked. Daddy Thee apologized for fussing at me. He wanted to ensure I had seen her and not waited as she had requested.

I said, "It's okay. I understand you were just checking, but I was there."

He replied, "Okay, baby girl, I'm sorry and love you." I told him I loved him too, and we hung up.

To know Daddy Thee is to love him. He was not angry at me because he was not being mean; on the contrary, he was very loving. Daddy Thee loved my mommy dearly; they had gone to school together. He expressed how he wanted to marry her when they were younger after she gave birth to me. But life and things happened, and they didn't marry then. Years later, after other failed marriages, they started dating again and got married. I was extremely happy; not only did I have a father in my life, but I also had one sister and two brothers.

I was happy that Daddy Thee stayed in my life all those years after they broke up. He treated me like family before we were officially family. He would check on me and Addie when I was growing up. Sometimes, he brought his children with him so we could play. They later became my siblings.

He was tall, chocolate, and hefty. He was a gentle giant who was serious for real about four things: his wife, family, money, and God. My daddy was what I call a thug pastor. He had a voice like an angel when he sang but was long-winded when he talked or preached. Daddy Thee's laughter was contagious. I loved him, and he loved us. Family was extremely important to him, and he ensured his wife's request was handled.

After the call with Daddy Thee, I continued to relax a bit before I started cleaning up to prepare for my mommy to come to my house the next day.

I will never forget the call I got about 30 minutes later. Even now, the thought of it still sends chills down my body and causes my heart to race a bit. I was sitting on my couch. When I heard the phone ringing, I thought it was my daddy again, but this time it was

Addie. She was screaming on the phone. At first, I could not understand what she was saying. The words and sounds were muffled.

Then it became clear, as her cry intensified, "She's dead! She's DEAD!"

I screamed back, "What? Who? Slow down! What is going on?" I screamed.

"Your mother. She is dead," is all Addie kept saying.

I dropped the phone in shock. In total disbelief, I shook my head, thinking, *this can't be happening. I just talked to her. I just saw her. She is coming over tomorrow.* "NO!" I screamed.

I grabbed my keys and ran out of the house to the car to rush over there. Then I realized I had no shoes on and no purse, so I went back inside to get them. As I was getting my shoes, Daddy Thee called me back to tell me he had called 911. My Mommy had stopped breathing, but she was not dead, and Addie was overreacting. I slightly calmed down at the sound of his voice and his words, but my heart was still racing and pounding in my ears from Addie yelling, "She's dead!"

I tried calling MX, but his line was busy. I had to get to the house quickly. With my keys in hand and, this time, wearing shoes, I ran out the door. I just drove as fast as I could. I don't remember any red lights and barely any vehicles. I went to his house first because I was distraught and needed him to keep our daughter, and I needed prayer; so many things swirling in my head, like a blizzard picking up speed; if it didn't stop, my mind was going to break. When I arrived, I banged on the door, crying desperately for someone to open the door quickly. When the door opened, I was so worked up that I could barely get the words out of my mouth. I finally caught my breath, and his mother asked, "What's going on?" His mother told me to take some deep breaths and tell her what happened. After praying for me, she told me that I couldn't help my mommy if I were hysterical. She encouraged me to remain calm.

I had to get to Addie's house quickly as that was where my mommy was. MX was there as well, and he insisted on going with me, although we drove separate vehicles. We drove separately because MX said he wasn't staying long and would have to leave. As we got to the intersection not too far from Addie's house, I could hear the blaring sound and see the ambulance's flashing lights. We saw the ambulance, and as it turned the corner in front of us, I saw my mother's face.

MX motioned for me to follow them. We followed the ambulance to the hospital. They ran traffic lights; we ran traffic lights. All I saw was them doing chest compressions while the siren blared. The paramedics were motioning for us to stop following them so closely. Despite their request, nothing would stop me from being within an eye's distance of my mommy.

She was in that ambulance, and I had to be where she was. As we approached the hospital, the ambulance was given space to pass by. But some cars would not let us in to stay near the ambulance as they turned off. They were blowing at us as if we were trying to bypass traffic. "NO," I screamed. Tears burst forth from my eyes even more.

Where is she? Where have they taken her? We had lost the ambulance. My heart sank deep into a pit of despair. My breathing had increased, and I was shaking. We drove for what seemed like an eternity because we had initially gone to the wrong area. We finally made it to the parking area of the main hospital and asked a security guard driving on a cart, "Where do the ambulances go?" and they pointed us in the right direction. We had to go left to the backside of the hospital and park near the emergency room.

Once parked and rushing to the ER doors, I saw my daddy Thee standing outside near the ambulance that my mommy had been in; I fell into his arms. He squeezed me tight. He said, "Pray and hold on, baby." *How? How do I hold on? My thoughts felt anxious.* But I mustered the strength because I believed in him.

Daddy Thee, MX., and I went inside, and one of the hospital staff took us into a room to wait for updates. A family friend who Daddy Thee had called to pray was there also. He and his wife wanted to be there in person. I looked around the room. It was small, cold, and dreary. No pictures on the wall, just a small empty end table to the side, with several chairs along the wall. The room was quiet as long as the door was closed. Only when someone came in from the waiting area could I hear the loud noises coming from there. Daddy Thee's friend told us that whenever they put you in a room like the one we were in, the person had died.

I yelled at him, "She is not dead; stop, stop saying that."

My daddy Thee grabbed me and said, "It's okay, baby. We are trusting God and waiting for the doctor." The family friend apologized for upsetting me; he only wanted to help us be prepared.

Soon after, our pastor came in and prayed with us. Daddy Thee had called him while on the way to the hospital. A nurse came in with tissues as she saw the end table was empty. She began talking to us about what had happened to my mommy's body and that this was normal with the disease. She quickly realized by the looks on our faces the doctor had not been in, and she abruptly stopped talking and left the room.

Our pastor went out to speak with her and then returned to speak with us. The pastor stated, "The doctor will be in shortly to give us more information."

But he confirmed that my mommy had passed away. Her heart stopped. At that moment, it was as though my heart stopped beating briefly. Silence consumed the room. No one was moving. I could hear my heart beating through my chest; it was a thunderous sound. I could feel the intensity grow as though it was about to explode. CRASH! My heart broke all over again. So many pieces shattered all over. How could I put it back together again?

I slumped over. Daddy Thee grabbed me in his arms. I cried. That's all I could do. MX patted my shoulder, unsure of what to do or say. The others' faces looked pained. I buried my head in Daddy Thee's chest and just cried. He was trying to be strong, but I felt his silent sobs as he held me. And a few warm tears from his face fell onto mine. Our pastor gave us words of encouragement, but he knew we needed to release the pain that was swelling deep inside of us.

God, WHY? She was a good person, a faithful servant, and a loving mother. We had just begun to repair the breach that Addie had left. We had just found our way back to one another completely as mother and daughter. *Why did you take her??* The tears would not stop falling, and I didn't try to stop them either. The doctor finally came in and explained that the disease had spread to her internal organs and hardened them. Ultimately, her heart and her lungs stopped functioning. The doctor asked if we wanted an autopsy done to confirm. I screamed at him, "NO! Don't you cut on my mommy!"

Daddy Thee squeezed me and told the doctor, "No, we don't want one."

The doctor nodded and said, "Once we clean her up, we will take you back to see her."

Then he left the room. It seemed colder now and a little more crowded as a few more people had come into the room to check on us and get an update on Mommy. No words were spoken, only the sounds of crying, feet moving, and shuffling in seats. The nurse came in and walked us to the back to see her. Daddy Thee and MX were on each side of me, and the others were behind us. When we got back to the room where her body lay, she was almost ice cold; her body was so thin and so frail. She didn't look like my mommy. The rosy color was no longer in her cheeks; her pretty brown hair was scarce, only pieces here and there. Her appearance had changed over time due to the disease. Her soft skin, which was light with a tint of red, as I liked to call it, had become dark, rough, and thick. This was not my mommy. After I kissed her on her cheek and told her goodbye, the tears stopped.

When I arrived back home alone, the first thing I saw was the birthday cake on my counter. The cake I never got to cut and share with my mommy. That birthday cake she had brought me sat for about 7-8 months after she passed. I could not bring myself to eat or throw it away; it was too painful. To cut the cake for me was like cutting myself with a sharp knife of regret. To throw it away was like discarding my mommy again. *Why did I ignore her request for a little piece of cake and a moment of time?* Because it was more important that MX saw it first. Even though she could not eat cake, she was willing to risk it for me. The disappointment on her face when I said I wanted to wait still haunts me. I had hurt her feelings, which was the last thing I wanted to do. Control is such a b****. The control that MX had combined with the controlling forces in that house made me susceptible and vulnerable. I was like a puppet on a string. Make me move, make me dance. There are so many things in life that I regret; not eating that one slice of cake with my mommy outweighs them all.

> *Mommy's death was a painful and hard pill to swallow. I didn't get to make right not taking the time to celebrate that last time with her. This established another layer of depression for me. I didn't celebrate my birthday or eat cake for almost 14 years after Mommy's death. As you reflect on this chapter, what are some things you wish you could change from your own experiences? What are some things you wished you would have said?*

No More Regrets - Reflection

What is something that you did or did not do that you still regret? Does it hinder your life's forward movement? Does it affect how you see things? Have you taken steps to change your thoughts and actions?

After thinking things over, do you do things differently now? Do you have difficult conversations? Do you make the time? Do you eat the cake? If not, what is stopping you? Change the narrative now so that you do not create more regret in your life. What can you do differently now to be more intentional?

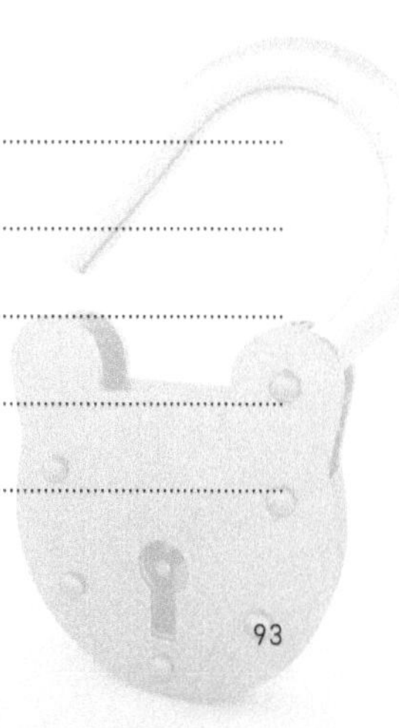

Chapter 10

Hollow-Not Going Back (Trigger Warning)

The faint sounds of the siren blaring in the background still haunt me. For months, I would wake up in a sweat, hearing the sirens and seeing them performing chest compressions as I followed the ambulance. Were the haunting memories why I was violently trembling, and were the pills that were in my hand a few moments ago missing? Were those memories why I was back in this house, the house where I had been traumatized as a child, beaten, harassed by demons, molested, and raped? I had made up my mind that this was where I planned to die. I was already dead mentally, emotionally, and spiritually - there was no reason to fight for a physical life tormented by trauma and pain. I wanted to die.

How can one person go through so much pain and heartache? The only thing I ever wanted was love. Why was that so hard to find? I hopelessly wondered why every turn seemed like I literally fell into a trap. Trapped and confined in my mind and my emotions, blinded by all of the pain, I could not see a way beyond my trauma. The swirling blizzard in my head dissipated somehow, and the image in the mirror that had become blurred now took form again. The inward battle was so strong. Do I fight or give up? My face was still streaked with tears. But I no longer felt like the eight-year-old cowering in a corner after being violated, the lost teenager looking for love in all the wrong places, or that young woman who got trapped deep in the spider's web.

I had evolved emotionally and mentally in what felt like a split second. Even though the home triggered traumatic memories, I was no longer the helpless little girl. Yes, I am her, but I am no longer physically in those moments from my childhood. I was 39 years old and back in that cold, full-size bed at Addie's house, staring at the shell of myself in the large, old, square, and termite-damaged mirror.

So many questions were going through my head. "*Would I ever stop crying? Would I ever stop hurting*?" I paused for a second and began to look around the room. As I peered at those bleak walls, it felt like my fate had been sealed. Addie always said that I would come back here to die just like my mommy. I shuttered at the thought, but now I was back at this house with no hope for the future and no rest from my discombobulated past. And just like that, my head was beaming with pain again. All those thoughts had come racing back. I wanted the thoughts and the pain to stop. I didn't want to feel the pain of my parents leaving me and being told they didn't want me, losing my grandfather, who was my champion, being molested as a child and blamed for what they did to me, having my heart broken by my first child's father, getting entangled in an abusive relationship, dealing with demonic attacks, and losing my mommy. The pain was too great.

Then suddenly, out of nowhere, the pills that were missing had reappeared in my hand. I got back in front of that mirror and started ranting with a vengeance. Except this time, I yelled at Addie. "You did this to me! You said I would come back here and die like my mother did!" I cursed at her for everything she had put me through. "You brought those men around me to hurt me! You let my grandaddy die! You kept me and my mommy apart for all those years, and now she is gone! I hate you! I HATE YOU!"

I detested her very being at that moment. I wished her dead, but she was already dead. I was persuaded that Addie was the one who had done this to me. She had cursed me. She spoke of me being back in this house to die, like my mother did, over me. I felt weak and powerless from what seemed like being under a spell. My head was spinning; my thoughts were still racing, and the weight of the memories was crushing my sanity. I was cold and by myself, but I didn't feel alone. Is this how the rest of my life would be - cold, confused, and lonely?

Even when I was in a crowd of people, I felt alone. No matter what I did or who I was around. I always seemed to feel ostracized, like I was not a part of what was happening or was not good enough to be there. My mind was always spiraling from one thought to another. Before I could capture one thought, here came another. I just wanted it to be over with. I wanted the chaos in my mind to stop. I needed it to cease; the pain was excruciating. Every fiber of my being was in torment and demanded relief. I wanted to be free! I needed consolation, but there was none in sight.

As I sat, I stared at the empty shell of a person I had become. *Who would love this? Who would want this?* My parents didn't want me, and neither did Addie, truthfully. Unloved, unwanted, unprotected, and deserted. I had been molested and pimped out at an early age, which led to sleeping with men in an attempt to feel loved and validated. Only to leave me with children out of wedlock. I love my babies, and I don't regret them at all. My dark places led me to an abusive and toxic relationship, which birthed emotional and mental breakdowns. Not to mention fighting for my life almost every night from whichever demon was trying to destroy me.

I was tired. Tired of fighting. Tired of trying. Tired of hoping. Tired of wishing. Tired of praying. *Would my life ever change? Could I find real love and no longer this false sense of love? Could someone actually love me through my brokenness?* I felt like the crackled glass that you see in the store. It's beautiful yet complicated. There are no defining lines. But if you look close enough and deep enough, you will see the beauty of what was once whole has been slightly shattered.

My life was the crackled, shattered glass; all I could see in me was brokenness. The crackled glass has a shattered appearance, but there is a beauty to it that most love and find intriguing, which is why they buy it. As for me, when I looked in the mirror, I saw no beauty, no love. Not even the person. In the brokenness, scattered moments of love held the broken pieces together. The love that was given and received at various times was beautiful. Unfortunately for me, the agony of loss and heartache drew the brokenness, not the beauty, to the forefront.

For years, I had become what others wanted me to be. I wore many masks to hide the broken pieces. Surely, if I saw it, they could have. I didn't even know who I was. My life was a lie. The real truth of who I was and what my life had been was too scary to accept or share. *Who would love that? Who would love me? Three, two, and one. I am tired, and I am almost done.* Looking at myself in the mirror, staring back at me, was a worn down and depleted woman who was hollow inside.

> *I was tired of being tired from everything I had gone through. We all have gotten to this place at some point. Look in the mirror. When were you tired of being tired? Don't force the thoughts; allow them to come as they choose. As the seasons of exhaustion come to mind, look for common threads and jot them down. Then, begin looking for strategies to change your season of being tired. We often want a quick resolution, and we don't have all the pieces to the puzzle because we have not taken the time needed to examine the problem.*

Empty Shell - Reflection

> *For in the day of trouble He will hide me in His shelter; In the secret place of His tent He will hide me; He will lift me up on a rock. - Psalms 27:5 (AMP)*

When you stop to look at your life from the earliest point you can remember, what relationship types, emotional struggles, or other crises have left you worn out? What are you tired of in this moment that you want to change? Where is there still pain in your life that you want relief from? Do you feel hollow and empty inside? Who or what caused you to feel this way?

Now that you have identified some things, realize you are not in those places anymore. Yes, you may still struggle with some things due to what happened in your past, but you are not in that space anymore. Your past does not have to define who you are and where you are going. Your past was a starting point for where your life began. You are still here; even among the hurt and the pain, you are still here. You get to choose how you move forward and what direction your life will take. What would you do differently now, knowing what you know and having taken the time to step back and look at things from a different perspective? Learn from the past and move differently. It's not too late.

> *This is my comfort and consolation in my affliction, That Your word has revived me and given me life. - Psalms 119:50 (AMP)*

See the crackled glass. What did you learn from it? How do you view it now? In the broken pieces of your life, can you still find beauty? Trace the lines to find the paths of love, honor, and respect. They are there. Look deeper.

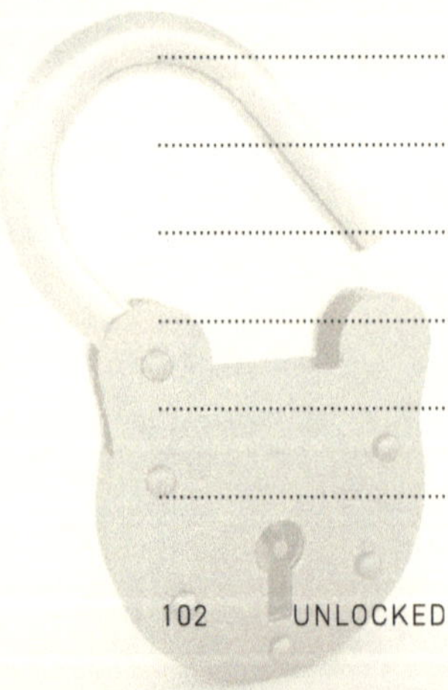

Chapter 11

Lock Down (Trigger Warning)

My mom's death brought on a new realm of emotional destitution and a sense of shame. I let my mother down for a man. A man who didn't care about me enough to spend my special day with me or even drive me to the hospital after hearing I received a call that my mother was dead. As I sat on the bed, I was beyond exhaustion from carrying the emotional weights wearing me down. *What am I going to do now?* My head was pounding, and my thoughts were racing - thoughts of regret, pain, bitterness, and helplessness. Reality came crashing in, with my mommy now gone; who did I have to lean on?

When Mommy became more stable in her life, she was more stable in mine. With stability finally present in our lives, she was there when I needed her and, at times, a great help with my children. We were starting to flow and have a greater relationship before she died.

Once my mommy died, the yelling, cursing, and physical abuse from MX kicked up a notch. I became more isolated from family and friends. He increasingly controlled and monitored what I could do, say, and wear. I was a prisoner on lockdown. Every move was scrutinized. My slightest mess-up meant I got hit.

I was scared to say the wrong thing or move the wrong way. It was a sinister game of Russian roulette. Would this trigger him or that? There was no sure way to know what he was thinking. Sometimes, he would blow up; other times, he would glare at me. It seemed to be the calm before the storm, almost like he was allowing things to build up so he could explode at a greater level.

Ring. Ring. Ring. The phone sounded off. I would shiver because I knew what was going to happen next. Immediately, the questions would start. Questions I couldn't respond to since I hadn't answered the call yet. "Who is that? What do they want? Why are they calling you?" MX would get so heated if I didn't have a good response. "I don't know," was all I could mutter. *I am not a psychic, so how the heck do I know who it is, what they want, or why they are calling me at that moment?* I wouldn't dare speak those thoughts for him to hear or say anything sarcastic, knowing that the ringing phone made his anger boil.

I would sometimes let the phone go to voicemail, only for MX to get in my face, breathing hard and yelling, "Call them back! What are you trying to hide? You must be up to something."

I could feel the hot and steamy anger coming through his pores. He towered over me as I shrunk down in fear. No, I was embarrassed and ashamed. *How did I allow myself to get caught up in this mania?* I couldn't have a conversation with whoever was calling because my voice would tremble. The caller would know that something was wrong.

MX would be glaring at me the whole time I was on the phone, still asking, "What do they want?"

Honestly, I never knew what most of those calling me wanted. I would focus on trying to rush them off the phone while trying to sound normal, even though I was scared about what might happen next.

You might say, why not leave him? I thought about it and made a few attempts, but where was I going? The true family that I had was gone, including my mommy. Granddaddy Ves had died, and my dad, Harold, was in another state. My daddy Thee tried to be there for me and help where he could, but he was still grieving. Even though being with MX was emotionally and physically abusive, I convinced myself that it was better than nothing. Had Addie's horrible relationship advice come true, "A piece of man is better than no man at all?" Oh, the horror. How had I succumbed to that? I knew better. Didn't I? I was so angry with myself for allowing this to happen to me.

As time passed, I became pregnant again from MX – the third time – despite continuing abuse. In 1998, we had our son; in 2005, we had another daughter. You would think after our first child, I would not have had to go through all the foolishness, but here we were yet again.

During my second and third pregnancies, he demanded, "You cannot have this baby; my family will be angry with me. You did it, fix it. You got to do something about not getting pregnant."

Last time I checked, it took two to have a baby. He didn't want to stop having sex with me, yet each time I got pregnant, he didn't want me to keep the baby. Many may say, why not get on birth control? Although I tried different types of birth control, I kept getting pregnant.

I didn't want to keep going through the rejection, the abandonment, the accusations, the blame, and the abuse. Something had to give; I couldn't keep bringing children into this world with this person. So, after I had my fifth child– my last one - I made the decision to have my tubes tied. It was a guaranteed way to avoid another pregnancy. The crazy thing is MX tried to talk me out of getting my tubes tied. He said if I got married, I wouldn't be able to have any more babies. He went as far as trying to persuade the doctor not to do the procedure. I was dumbfounded. What the hell? Thankfully, he had no say in the matter since we were not married. How could he even say that I shouldn't get my tubes tied? Each time I got pregnant, the story had the same lines. "It is not the right time." "My family would be mad." "It's all your fault," and all the other foolishness he spouted. I was going to tie my tubes and not birth any more children from him. I was already a single mother to five children for whom I was responsible. It would be unfair to me and to them to have any more and not have any tangible, consistent help.

A couple of years before my second daughter was born, there was a situation with my first-born son that ultimately resulted in him going to live permanently with his father. This was exceedingly difficult for me. I always felt that if I loved him enough, he would love me back and not leave me. His actions and behaviors in the household were causing chaos, and the police were called.

My son stole shoe polish and then ran away. When he came back home, he was disciplined. MX tore his butt up, and I did too. Unknowingly, he had welts on his behind and didn't tell me. He decided to call the police instead while I was out. I later found out that he had called them initially to get MX locked up, but it resulted in me going to jail instead. I was so broken and upset. I sent him to live with his dad, thinking maybe that would be better for him. MX was fine with the decision; one less person for him to deal with.

In the relationship with MX, there were times when the sex was not consensual. He didn't ask me to have sex or even engage in romantic talk or foreplay to entice me to want to have sex with him. If I resisted or said I didn't want to, he would force me into the room and make me take my clothes off. A few times, he hit me and dragged me to the room forcefully. He didn't care about what I wanted or what God wanted.

He would yell, "What did I say? I don't care what you want!"

"But what about what God wants?" I asked once.

The words that came out of his mouth next sent chills down my spine, and I ducked.

"I don't care about what God wants! I said it's my way or no way!"

He almost growled when he said it. I knew he was going to get struck by lightning. Heck, let's be honest; I was hoping he *would* get struck by lightning. But nothing dramatic like that occurred; he kept yelling about what he wanted, how it was going to be, and how he didn't care how I felt.

He wouldn't allow me to leave. He had control and power. Our relationship would not be over until he said it was over. Time after time, I tried to leave. But he wasn't having it. On one occasion, he even swung a hammer at my head.

He shouted, "I will put you six feet under right next to your mama."

As I looked at him in horror, I could discern he was not playing. How could he be so cold? My mother had not even been dead six months then. The grief and regret were still weighing heavy on me. His words were a crushing blow to my heart.

Our children were standing there when he spoke those horrible words to me. I didn't want them to see or hear anything else, so I sent them to their rooms. Hurt and angry at his words, I snapped at him before I knew it. "I don't want to be with you anymore, and I definitely don't want to marry you one day," I screamed.

Before I could say anything else, a knife was at my throat as I held our last child in my arms; she was not even one yet. So many things flashed before my eyes. Thoughts of him stabbing me, him accidentally stabbing our daughter who I was holding, screaming for help, and the kids coming to my rescue, and him stabbing them also. I was visibly shaking.

The last thing I wanted was for my children to come out of their rooms and find their mother lying in a pool of her own blood on the kitchen floor. So, even as scared as I was, I played nice and said what he wanted me to say so that he would calm down and step back. With tears in my eyes, I told him I was sorry and wouldn't leave him. I assured him that he was very important to me and that I would listen to him. He then lowered the knife from my throat, but it remained in his hands.

The coldness from the hollow of his eyes was gripping as he stared at me. He had said many things before and would make threats, but the look he had as he held that knife to my throat was bone-chilling. I knew my life would be over if I said the wrong word.

He wanted me to prove I was not lying to him. He wanted me to have sex with him to prove that I meant what I said. How do you go from threatening a person's life to having sex with them? Help me understand that. I guess that's what he meant when he said it was his way or no way. MX wanted what he wanted and had better get it, or there would be consequences to pay for not complying. So, if he wanted sex, he got it. I would be so sick to my stomach as he pounced up and down on me. Many times, I would go to the bathroom afterward and throw up and cry. That day when he threatened my life was no exception. I was so frightened I didn't know if he would come back and still slit my throat.

I was petrified. I wanted out of the relationship hell I was in. But how? Saying I was abused is an understatement. I was abused, tortured, tormented, threatened, ridiculed, shamed, and broken. Every part of me went through trauma. My physical, emotional, spiritual, sexual, and mental capacities were mangled, depleted, and drained. I felt like a worthless rag doll being tossed around, banged into things, dragged through the mud, and run over by a Mack truck. I was trapped. I felt as though I was in prison with no way of escape. Several times, I tried to leave, but the pull that he had on me was so strong. He controlled my every move. He was the warden. I was his prisoner.

With all that I had gone through, I began to change—the friendly people person I once was had checked out. I had become withdrawn. The girl, once a social butterfly, began isolating herself from social events. Why get close to anyone when he would make me stop talking to them? I didn't trust people. I had severe anxiety issues; at times, I would leave a full cart of groceries in the middle of the aisle because I would suddenly become fearful about what was going to happen next.

I had nervous breakdowns, meltdowns, suicide attempts, extreme depression (manic and bipolar), and slight schizophrenia (that's what the doctors diagnosed me with). After years of hearing an array of psychological terms, I ended up being diagnosed with Post-Traumatic Stress Disorder (PTSD). Working, trying to raise my five children (three of which were his), and pretending as if everything were okay was all so draining. But I had to keep up the pretense for his image and to hide my shame. I could not let others know what he was doing to me behind closed doors. He had an image to uphold. I wore many masks during that time, and I didn't know who I was anymore. I had become lost, devoured by the once pretty web that spun lies, deceit, broken promises, and pain.

Many people think only prisoners of war (POW) who had been locked up, tortured, and beaten go through PTSD once they are released from their capturer. Many don't make it to freedom, even once they have been released. Their minds break down from the weight of the pressure, and even though their physical bodies are free, their minds are trapped in a cycle of torture and brokenness.

I can identify with them. All the years of his abuse - verbal, physical, mental, sexual, and spiritual, coupled with Addie's abuse broke my psyche. My PTSD, like that of many others, developed from having experienced something shocking, scary, or dangerous. This can happen to anyone who has gone through minor or severe traumas. And it can develop after one event or continuing events. There is help. Seek counseling with a therapist who specializes in or deals with traumas. Having a trauma-centered therapist will aid you in the process of getting to the root of the problem and digging it up.

> *I had never pictured myself in a violently abusive situation. These types of things happened on TV and to others, not to me. But I had fallen prey, and it almost cost me my life. Have you ever been so lost in someone or something that you no longer recognize yourself? As you begin your time of reflection, sit and really think about this question.*

Imprisoned-Reflection

> *Casting all your cares [all your anxieties, all your worries, and all your concerns, once and for all] on Him, for He cares about you [with deepest affection, and watches over you very carefully].*
> *-1 Peter 5:7(AMP)*

Have you ever been in a relationship (any type of relationship) where your thoughts, feelings, cares, and concerns didn't matter? The other person (or people) in the relationship bulldozed over you any chance they got. They made you feel safe one minute and violated the next. This may be hard to admit. But sit down and think about it. It may have started small and then grew over time. You lost your voice. You lost your choice. How did it make you feel? Were you able to get it back? Are you still fighting to get it back?

You matter! Your voice matters! Your thoughts and opinions matter! Take some time and read the affirmations listed aloud. As you begin to say them, begin to feel them. Then add to the list as confidence becomes your portion.

I am not a mistake. I have a purpose, and I am fulfilling it.
I have value. I am loved by God, and I love myself.
I am worthy.
I am no longer broken. God is making me whole.
I am accepted in the beloved. I am God's chosen vessel.
I am fearfully and wonderfully made.
I am not hopeless. I am hopeful, and I can do what I put my mind to.
I am strong. Even when I may feel weak, there is strength within me.
I will not give up on me. I will fight and continue to move forward into my purpose.
My voice matters. I will not be silent.

Use this link to do an online PTSD screening. Once you have your results and if it is determined you have PTSD, seek counsel to get the proper help for you.
https://www.mcleanhospital.org/screening-ptsd

Getting help and seeing a therapist is not a bad thing. You need help walking through some issues and traumas and processing them to get to a better place. Here are links to help you get started in finding the help that you deserve:

https://therapyforblackgirls.com/
https://www.melaninandmentalhealth.com/
https://www.betterhelp.com
https://www.growtherapy.com
https://findtreatment.gov/
https://www.psychologytoday.com/us/therapists

You have the power to take your life back. Getting help is a start to that process. You have a choice: find the professional who is the right fit for you. Don't be one-and-done. Your life and future are on the line.

Chapter 12

Bottomed Out - But God

Finally, after 15 long years, I got the courage to leave MX and do bad all by myself. That day felt like the worst day ever because I didn't know where I would live or lay my head. That day also felt like the best day of my life because I was free. God, You did it! You gave me the strength and power to say enough, NO MORE. I'm done! My hope for better was slowly starting to return. Every shackle that held me bolted down fell off. I was free to go where I wanted. Talk to others without guilt and shame. I would soon find peace again, joy again. It was time to learn to love me because years of abuse had created a warped sense of love.

Who would have known how much leaving him would cost me? My son and I were kicked out of his parents' house after having lived there for months. Confusion arose concerning my work schedule, his mom keeping the youngest daughter all day and the other three after school, and other issues. He was not helping with the kids because he was too busy stalking me at my job after he got off of work. This caused his mom to have long days with the children. But having to leave his parents' house and realizing MX had contributed to his parents' decision to ask me to leave made getting and staying out more plausible.

Leaving also meant that I had to leave my three youngest children behind with MX's parents. I did this because I had nowhere to go, and I did not want my kids sleeping on the streets. Still, I had nowhere for my second son and me to go after we were put out of MX's family home. I tried to find him a place to stay. I had even begged Addie to allow him to stay with her until I could get a place for us, but she refused. I had to drag my son with me during this tumultuous time. He was a trooper through all of the ups and downs, never complaining, just taking it all in stride. Looking back, I can see he was suppressing his emotions and anger. I was so caught up in my trauma that I had not realized the traumatic effect that it had and was having on him at the time. If only I could go back and protect him and comfort him the way he deserved.

For a little while, the two of us lived in my storage unit. We had nowhere else to go except that storage unit. It was a large unit and held all of our belongings from my old three-bedroom apartment. I set things up for us to be as comfortable as possible. We had a recliner and a hard white plastic chair, like people use at picnics, to sleep on. I arranged our suitcases up front so we could easily get to our clothes. There was a plug on the outside of the unit so that I could charge my phone at night. We had to wait until the office closed so they would not know we were there. I would put the code in, so the alarm didn't go off. We would go inside and get settled in. I had a pillow and blanket for both of us. I would pull the large aluminum door down and rest it on a small suitcase, leaving a small opening along the bottom. This was so we could get some air and so no one would know we were in there. We would get up early in the morning and go across the street to the bus station to wash up and get ready for the day. His school was close enough but still some distance away from the storage place. Most days, he would walk to school and catch the bus to my job to wait for me to get off so we could return to the storage unit together. No one initially knew we were staying there except for MX. He offered to get me a hotel room for one night, but it was only so we could have sex, and then I could bring my son there to sleep afterward. I declined his insulting offer.

I had little money, no car, no home, and no one I could call for help. All we had was each other and our belongings in a storage unit. Still, we made it work. For a few weeks, we were able to stay at my godmother's house temporarily and then at a friend's place for a few days. Because MX was obsessed with controlling me, he was not letting my decision to leave go lightly. He harassed me constantly at my job by calling repeatedly, coming to the store, and standing around watching me work while trying to talk to me. He didn't know where we were staying as he had been looking for us at the storage unit. I would never reveal our location because I didn't want him harassing me or the ones who allowed us to stay with them temporarily. He called my phone incessantly to the point I would turn it completely off so that I could get some peace of mind. He called all day long; sometimes, he would call 20-30 times back-to-back as if that would make me answer the phone. Finally, I would turn it off. MX would always tell me that I could not make it without him. Oh, but God always makes a way.

And I held onto this even in the midst of the struggles. I had a hope that somehow, some way, one day, things would get better for me and my kids.

I had prayed that God would make a way for me to care for my children without needing MX's family's assistance. They were the ones who actually took care of the children. I held onto the hope of experiencing what real love was and finding it. Finding the person who would care for me, understand me, help me be a better person, and love me unconditionally.

After almost four months of being asked to leave our temporary home, I thankfully got back on my feet and got an apartment with some help. My pastor at the time, who was also my aunt, found out that my son and I were sleeping in a storage unit. She didn't feel it was safe for us to stay there, so she allowed us to stay with her for a month. She got me a new job, making more money. She also helped me find an apartment I could afford and paid the deposit so I could get in quickly and get my other three children back.

Since I didn't have a car, two ladies from the church I was attending, who were like family to me, took me to get my kids and their things. When we arrived in two cars, we discovered all the kids' things were sitting in the driveway of their grandparents' house. They did it to me rudely, but it made packing up the cars quick and easy. I had no desire to step foot back in their house for anything. His mother stood there looking sour at us as we packed the cars. I said thank you to his dad, and we left. MX was not home when we retrieved the kids, for which I was grateful. Not because I would have caved in and gone back to him, but because I didn't want his drama or him trying to follow us to where we lived. My babies were so excited.

Our place was a small two-bedroom, one-bath apartment, but it worked, and it was ours. I was so happy to have my babies back home with me. To have our own place again was wonderful. The boys were in one room, and the girls slept in the other room with me. To be able to sit and laugh with them again was truly a blessing. I had worked so hard to get to this place. My older daughter told me one day when I visited her at her school that all she wanted for her birthday was to be back with me and all of us living together again. I didn't make it by her birthday in March, but we did have our own place by April before they went on Spring break.

Once I left MX, and before I got my children back, I developed a deeper relationship with God. In the past, it was religion and habit to go to church. I knew of God but didn't have a real relationship with Him. But I longed to get up early and pray. I could not wait to talk to Him and hear what He wanted me to do differently. I yearned for real love. Not just sex or the empty words, "I love you," from a man, but I wanted to experience true agape (unconditional) love. I read my Bible more and asked God to show me what real love was and what His love looked like. I wanted real love and no longer trusted my judgment to find it.

With God's help, I made it on my own. My life changed for the better in so many ways. Not only were the kids and I at peace in our own place, but I was able to reconcile with my oldest son. And God sent a new man into my life. Not any old joker, but a real man.

Actually, he (John) was not so much new as he was old. Old in the sense that we had known each other before and had been friends. He is my good and perfect gift from God. John has been and still is a treasure to me. He always knew how to make me laugh and feel at ease. The feeling was still the same even though time, distance, and other relationships had played a factor.

We first ran into each other on the city bus some years before while I was still with MX. We talked for a bit, exchanged Myspace account information, and then left. We were friends who had known each other since I was around 15. There was nothing inappropriate going on. We talked here and there on Myspace (which was like the original social media site), but then, when MX found out about my Myspace account and that I had been communicating with John there, he blew up. I had to stop contact with John.

A year and a half later, I had broken up with MX and was on my own. The kids and I had our own place, and after several months, I had internet service and could get online again. I sent John a message to say hello and let him know that I was internet-friendly again. He responded hours later, asking, "Are you John-friendly?" He also asked, "If I give you my number, will you call me?" I laughed aloud and typed – "yes." After all, we were friends, and having a normal adult conversation was what I needed. Plus, he could make me laugh, and laughter was also definitely needed.

In August, about six and a half months after I left MX, John and I began to talk more regularly. At first, I dismissed him from being anything more than a friend. As the conversation progressed, we began to talk about relationships and what we wanted in that "special person." I opened up and shared a lot of things that I had longed for. Such as someone to love me, protect me, care for me in a pure and honest way, and love my children as their own.

John listened intently. And when the opportunity presented itself, he asked, "What about me?"

Shocked by the question, I responded, "What about you?"

As soon as the words left my mouth, I felt the Lord rebuke me, saying, "So, you put Me in a box? Haven't you been praying for a husband, a real man to love you? How do you know he is not my chosen one?" Immediately, I was stunned and ashamed of the thought of boxing God in. I had been praying, and I had a long, detailed list of what I wanted in a husband. What was I thinking? I repented to God and to John. I could hear the smirk through the phone as I told him I was sorry for dismissing him and putting God in a box. "I will let God be God, and we will see," I said.

He replied, "Oh, you gonna be my wife, wait and see." *That was a cocky comment*, I thought as I laughed slightly.

Little did I know God was doing a new thing. John was always a gentleman, and he made me feel special. Our first date was at his place. He had a one-bedroom apartment. Neither of us had a car then, so he rented a car and picked me up at church, where we agreed to meet. We both had busy schedules, so the plan was to come to get me after choir rehearsal for our date. He stopped at Burger King and allowed my kids to order whatever they wanted. Then we dropped them back off at my apartment before going to his place. During this time, my second son and oldest daughter were old enough to be at home alone with the other children for a few hours.

Only because I trusted John did I allow what happened next. Since he only had a one-bedroom apartment, he didn't want me to see anything until it was fully prepared. He blindfolded me and led me to his bedroom. Sneaky, sneaky. He had me take my shoes off, lay on his bed facing the window, and promised not to peek out the door until he came to get me. I promised, took the blindfold off, and played on my phone. I had to trust him as he led me straight to the bedroom on our first date - our inside joke. Once he had heated our dinner and prepared the table, he made me close my eyes as he led me to the table. When I opened them, I was in shock, in a good way. The table was set for two: wine, candlelight, a long-stemmed red rose at my place setting, and a greeting card. I wanted to cry. It was so beautiful.

No one had ever done anything like that for me. I had done it before for others, but having someone take the time to pamper me and make me feel special was overwhelming. I could barely eat my food.

He kept smiling at me, asking, "Are you okay?"

I smiled and answered, "Yes." I was so close to tears, but I couldn't let him see me cry. I had to be strong. It was too soon to let him know he had me. Then he gave me another card just because. I had to breathe through it because I almost cried. Mommy and I used to get and give cards to one another to show our love. He touched a place so deep in my heart that I didn't know could still be touched. After dinner, he played music, and we danced in his living room. It was the perfect night - our night. We had other dates, and some included the kids. But no matter what we did, we had fun and enjoyed one another.

God definitely did a new and quick thing in a matter of months. Six months, to be exact. Only God! We had become the Black Brady Bunch. I had five kids, and he had four. Before that, I prayed for God to send me a man who would love my kids as his own.

God stopped me mid-prayer one day with this question, "What if he has kids? Will you love them as your own also?" God has a way of getting to you. I paused for a moment. I had never thought about that, but as quickly as He asked the question, I responded, "Yes, God. I will love them as my own, and I pray that you would knit our hearts together when we meet." God did just that. As I met and hugged each of his children, I felt God knitting their hearts to mine. God is truly a promise keeper.

God will give you what you need and sometimes what you want. John has always been a good person. I only looked at him as a friend at first for varying reasons. One, he was shorter than me. I wanted a tall, dark, and handsome man. He is short but still dark and handsome. Also, I dated his best friend years prior (no judging). We all met at the same time, but his friend was more outspoken, so I dated him. Yet John and I became friends, and we had a connection that later would become known. Although he could make me laugh, his goofiness was annoying at times, but I soon came to love his goofiness and pettiness (which is still annoying sometimes). And the kids always remind me, "You married him."

I married him six months to the day we started talking. As I looked over the list of what I had been praying to God for, I saw that John was all that and more. He was not just what I wanted; he was what I needed. He helped me become better. He always challenges me to be better and supports me in whatever endeavor I wish to pursue. He is a dream come true.

To be honest, he scared me. I was so used to dysfunction and abuse that when God actually answered my prayers with a good man, a real man, I was waiting for the other shoe to drop. *You can't really be this nice. You are not this calm all the time. Do you ever raise your voice and yell?* He was like an enigma to me. There was always yelling in my house growing up as a child. With John, I was the only one yelling in our home because that was not his character at all. That took getting used to. And when I made a mistake, I would, out of habit, shrink back in fear of being yelled at or hit. He often reminded me, "I am not him; you are safe." *What was safe?* Being safe was foreign to me. I don't think I had ever felt safe with anyone except for both of my grandaddies, Sylvester and Ulysses, and my Daddy Thee. I wasn't around my dad (Harold) enough to know whether I felt safe with him or not.

My husband did his best daily to make me feel safe, loved, desired, and appreciated. My toxic past would sometimes try to sabotage the things that he was trying to do. But John never gave up on me. He still saw me as the cute little girl he had met in the church basement all those years ago. I wish I could see myself how he saw me. I felt so far from a cute, innocent church girl. I had so many scars, deep-rooted scars that cut me into two people. A woman who wanted to be loved and a woman who feared becoming vulnerable enough to love. You see, my scars were not cute or pretty. These ugly scars made me second guess or question John's love for me. I did my best not to make him pay for the abuse of others, but to be honest, I did not do a particularly good job. If he said something or did something that triggered me, I would blow up. I would yell, shut down, sometimes go into another room, and stay away from him. But God. In all we had gone through, a lesser man would have packed his things and left.

Not John. He prayed, and he trusted God that things would work out. He told me when we got married, "No matter what you do, I will not leave you." As sweet and crazy as that sounded, I didn't believe him. There was no way someone could really mean what he was saying. I was waiting for the day he would be proven a liar. Sometimes, I would do little things to test him. Mainly because I didn't feel worthy to have him as my husband; he was a good man, and I was a scared woman. I didn't know just how deep my scars from the past were until I was challenged to love through them. I didn't understand triggers and what I needed to do when they happened until God answered my prayers and sent me my husband. He encouraged me to get the help that I needed to get better and be better. All I knew was that this was supposed to be different, and being with John was different than any other relationship I had had before. God had done it. He had given me a miracle by giving me John. Little by little, I was being healed. I just didn't know it yet.

> *It was a fight to get out of that horrible relationship with MX. But once I let go, God gave me who and what I needed. As you begin to reflect, take time and look at who or what you may be holding on to that hinders you from the new thing you have been asking for.*

Ram in the Bush — Reflections

> *and provide for those who grieve in Zion— to bestow on them a crown of beauty instead of ashes, the oil of, joy instead of mourning, and a garment of praise instead of a spirit of despair. They will be called oaks of righteousness, a planting of the Lord for the display of his splendor. -Isaiah 61:3 (New International Version, NIV)*

When you have been at your lowest and don't know how you will get out, that's when God steps in and provides a ram in the bush or a way of escape. At the present time, it may not seem like a way of escape. But once you get out of it and look back over how things unfolded, you can see the hand of God. Getting kicked out was a blessing. It was the push I needed to get out of that toxic relationship with MX and make room for a new and better one. God had to make me uncomfortable to make me comfortable.

What situations have you been in that you should have left but didn't for whatever reason? How did you respond when things began to turn ugly and you were forced to leave? Think about what came after.

Can you see now that God was working things out for your good? What other things in your life right now do you need to let go of to make room for the new? What has God been telling you to release that you are still holding on to?

Chapter 13

Slipping into a Deep Slumber (Trigger Warning)

The relationship between John and I was supposed to be different. This relationship was supposed to be better. All my troubles, worries, and pain were supposed to leave. *'Why? Why would you do this to me?* I was hurt, and my mind was in turmoil. I screamed until I was almost hoarse as I glared into the tattered mirror that seemed to be taunting me again—tears gushing from my eyes. I had been crying for what seemed like days, yet it was only hours. How did I have any fluid left in my body? The living room had grown darker and colder. I was back in the room at Addie's house. Sitting all alone on the bed. The only glimmer of light was from the moon outside, peeking in through the curtains.

"God, why? You set me up with false expectations just to fail me. Making me think and believe that John could love me, flaws and all." I could barely muster these words out through the sobs and the drugs and alcohol that were setting in. A pop here and a sip there. My thoughts were all over the place. *What's the use of trying anymore? You are a failure and a loser, and everything else that Addie had said about you.* My eyes were getting heavy, but that didn't stop my ranting. My venom shifted from God to me. "You are going to hear me and listen good," I yelled to the dismal image in the mirror. "You are weak and pathetic! You had a good man, yet you could not keep him either. You are damaged goods. No one wants you; they all will be better off without you in their lives. You mess up everything that you touch. Just end it already." I was crushed and devastated.

The words pierced my heart and my soul. As I looked over what had been my life, it was worthless. Mistake after mistake, let down after let down, failure after failure. What good had I accomplished? It wouldn't make a difference if I was here or not. Everyone was mad at me or had an attitude toward me, and the one person who I thought would be on my side no matter what left me feeling high and dry.

I know it may seem trivial and stupid, but a promise is a promise. He promised that no matter what happened to us or how angry either of us got, he would never sleep on the couch. Granted, I had left the room a few times, but that was me spiraling out of control and not knowing how to explain what was going on. This time, he left and slept on the couch. No words, not even a glance back my way. That was the straw that broke me. I was already teetering on the edge. The old thoughts from rejection came back. He must hate me, too.

My mind was a swirling snowstorm with no visibility in sight. I was trapped in my mind, and at every turn, I was being bombarded by objects and blows. I could barely get a grip from one hit when another would come. There was no cover or end in sight; the blows kept coming. The pain was excruciating. "Make it stop, please make it stop," were my muffled cries for help. But no one heard me. No one came to my rescue. No one saw me.

Then, suddenly, it was clear. I had a plan, or so I thought it was my plan. *Just leave and end it all. You will save everyone else pain and heartache. Your kids will be better off without you; they don't listen to you half the time anyway. Your husband will be happier and won't have to sleep on the uncomfortable couch or deal with your emotional roller coaster.* This is what I was hearing in my head. It was ringing ever so loudly and on repeat like a broken record.

Out of the blizzard came calm and instructions. The plan was put into motion. I drafted three separate emails: one to my husband, one to my mentor, and one to my counselor. The plan was to send the emails once everything was in place after I had left. By the time they saw the emails, I would be gone. Freedom at last!

I got up early and went to Walgreens to fill my prescription. Then, I sat in the grocery store's parking lot until the liquor store next to it opened to get me a bottle of gin. I stopped by the graveyard where Addie was buried, and I cursed her out. I let her have it! I said everything I ever wanted to say but was either too afraid to say or not allowed to say. I cried, yelled, screamed, and cried some more before I finally drove off. I'm sure that if anyone were passing by, they would have thought I was crazy yelling at her grave the way that I was. I had to have that release.

I went to Addie's house and put the pills and the gin in the kitchen. I grabbed a handful of pills and put them in my pocket. I set up the front of the house in a way that no one would be able to tell I was there. I went to the Center for Manifestation, our church, next. Not to pray, oh no. I was far beyond prayer. I was responsible for an appointment at the church's Empowerment House; someone was coming to do a safety inspection. Since I didn't want to let anyone else down, I fulfilled that assignment as I prepared for what was the inevitable. However, it made no sense to keep the appointment, considering what I was about to do. In my mind, it was that one last act of kindness.

I went back home, but John was there and still not speaking to me. He barely looked at me when I came inside. He had worship music blasting and scriptures from his Bible app playing throughout the house. I locked myself in the bathroom to think and continue executing the plan. The worship and The Word playing loudly were excruciating to hear. That which used to soothe me was causing me agony. I can remember hitting my head against the wall, wanting it to stop. It hurt my ears. I began to get extremely agitated. It was as if my skin was crawling and needles pricking at me.

I needed to move fast. I checked the bus route and grabbed some cash for the bus fare. I only took the one key off my key ring to return to Addie's house. I left my wedding rings, phone, and keys on the nightstand and walked out of the house. I didn't even look back. For what? There was nothing there for me anymore.

As I hurried down the sidewalk, I ran into my bonus son as he walked home. "Are you ok?" he asked.

"Yes," I replied in a not at all convincing tone.

"Where are you going?" He asked.

"Just for a walk," I replied quickly. *Why does he keep asking me all these damn questions? Go home already.*

"You want some company?" He insisted.

"No. I am good; I just want to walk for a bit. I will be back soon," I said, hoping to sound sincere so he would leave. I quickly walked away, and I glanced back every now and then to make sure that he was walking the other way. He was looking back at me as well. As soon as I hit the corner, in my head, I heard "RUN!"

So, I did. As fast as I could to get around the other corner to get to the bus stop. And to my surprise, the bus came earlier than expected. I was so happy. The last thing I needed was for him to see me at the bus stop, come over, and start questioning me again.

On the bus, I felt a little relief. I had gotten away. I went to the library first to send the emails. I only needed the computer for a hot second. The emails were ready; they just needed to be sent—another delay in the plan. I had forgotten my library card. I asked the librarian if I could use the computer, explaining that I rushed out of the house and left my card. She was nice enough to give me a temporary login. I logged in for a minute, sent the emails in my draft, logged out, and left. I walked over to Burger King to get a bite to eat. I knew that I was about to take all those prescription pills; I needed to have something in my stomach. Also, I needed something to drink to add the gin to. I popped a few prescription pills while waiting for the bus to come.

Final Destination

The next bus came, and I was on my way. When I got off, I walked quickly to the house. I didn't need any of Addie's old, nosy neighbors watching me, trying to figure out what I was doing. I went through the back of the house and ensured nothing looked disturbed. This was key, so by the time my family found me, it would be too late. The other side of the house, where I used to stay and where my mommy died, would be my final destination.

As I sat in the dark, stale, and cold room of Addie's house, the smell of mothballs was in the air. The front door was a thick, heavy wooden one that sealed the room like a lid to a coffin. A full-size bed sat against the wall in the living room, a resting place of sorts. In the corner was a burnt orange swivel chair made of crushed velvet material. Its color had faded over time. Then there was the mirror; it was large, old, and square, and the wood was black with termite damage and scratches. There was other old wooden, rotting furniture in the room, but it all blurred in comparison to the burnt orange swivel chair, the mirror, and the bed I sat on.

With tears still streaming down my face, I dragged that ugly, worn, burnt orange chair over to the bed and placed the tattered mirror in it before me. I wanted to see; I needed to see. What was I looking for? I didn't really know, but I needed answers. I had to confront what was devouring me. The pain was excruciating.

I diverted my eyes from the mirror momentarily. Looking down, I realized the bottle of muscle relaxers that I had just gotten refilled was gripped in my hands, and a Burger King cup with gin and juice was on the floor next to my feet. The room, by this point, was closing in on me. I felt trapped. There was no turning back. As I sipped, swallowed, and cried, I looked up to God and, with as much intensity and vigor as I could manage, yelled, "You better not save me this time! I'm done, do you hear me? I'm done!"

I slumped over, crying and intoxicated. The room was getting blurry, but the pain was still strong. So, I took more pills and drank more gin in hopes the pain would soon be over. I looked into the mirror and yelled at the figment of myself. I would yell and pass out, then yell and pass out again. Each time I got up, the pain seemed greater instead of lesser. So, the more the pain, the more pills I took. I wanted to be dead to my feelings, dead to my pain, dead to my emotions. Just dead. As I was slipping into a deep slumber, I wondered if they would even bother to have a funeral for me. Who would come? No one cared enough about me anyway - the ones who did had already died. I was alone.

I felt alone and thought I was alone, but unbeknownst to me, I had a champion fighting for me. As I was slipping away, he was taking action.

> *I just wanted it all to be over. Have you ever gotten to that point when, no matter what you do, nothing seems to go right? And there is so much pain you want it all to go away. Take your time as you reflect and journal here about getting up to fight one more time and how you'll fight differently.*

The End — Reflection

> *Search me [thoroughly], O God, and know my heart; Test me and know my anxious thoughts; And see if there is any wicked or hurtful way in me, And lead me in the everlasting way. Psalms 139:23-24 (NIV)*

Have you ever had thoughts like, *What's the use? Why bother? Nobody cares. They don't understand.* How far did your thoughts go during those moments? Were the pain and the thoughts ever so great that to find peace, you considered sleeping the pain away?

Our words have power. Saying something just to say something or saying something out of frustration can cause us to deal with things we don't want to or cannot handle.

In a moment of frustration, saying, "I would rather die" or saying, "I would be better off not being here," opens a door in your mind for increased thoughts of worthlessness and sometimes suicidal thoughts. It can appear initially as a random thought, but it can become more frequent if we are not careful of the words that we speak. Think of a time when those thoughts came to your mind. What did you do? What was going on around you? Were the thoughts even true?

If you are still having these thoughts and you cannot shake them, get help. Some things, as I have said before, require help to process and overcome. Asking for and seeking professional help does not make you weak. On the contrary, it makes you stronger than you believe. Seeking help is the first step on your road to recovery and healing.

Chapter 14

John's Point of View

I sensed that something was off. Something was wrong. However, I couldn't grasp the extent or magnitude of how much things were awry. At one point, I began searching the entire house for you—inside, meticulously going through every room, the garage, and even outside. Malcolm was on his way home when he inquired, "What's going on? Are you okay?" I responded, "I am looking for Tina," to which he replied, "I passed her on the way."

I hopped into the car and initiated a search, navigating up and down different streets and exploring the routes you might have taken. My mind was scattered, and my emotions were in disarray. I knew there was a period before when you had left, and the uncertainty of your whereabouts was nerve-wracking. There was no note or any indication. This was not the first time this had happened, but it was still scary. Last time, as time passed,

I decided to contact the sheriff, although I was unsure of what action they would take. I had always heard that they wouldn't actively search for people until a 24-hour period had elapsed or something like that. Surprisingly, they did start looking for you, canvassing different places until they eventually located you. At that time, it was somewhat upsetting and a little unsettling.

This time was nerve-wracking. I noticed you left the keys, the phone, and the rings. Panic set in, evolving into fear. Shortly after I assumed the email was sent, the phone rang, and it was Sister Tillman, your mentor, asking, "What is going on? I got an email from Tina, and it makes no sense."

"I really don't know," I replied. "She left all her stuff here and has been gone for some hours." I informed her that our son had crossed her path up the street, but afterward, he didn't know where she went.

My son said, "If I had known and focused more, feeling something was going on, I wouldn't have let her just pass by and keep going."

However, he couldn't have known. He did go back toward where you were walking, but once he reached the corner, you were nowhere to be seen. So, he turned around and walked home.

I hung up the phone with her to see if you left me anything. And there was the email. I don't remember everything it said. I remember a couple of things: you wanted to be a good wife, never intending to but wanting to make my life better, not worse. And that I'll be better off without you, or everyone would be better off without you.

Be Free

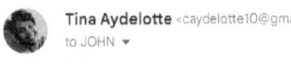

Tina Aydelotte <caydelotte10@gmail.com> Wed, Sep 26, 2012, 2:58 PM
to JOHN

John,

You are now free to be the man God called you to be without any further hindrances from me or the children. You are a good man I just was not the right person for you. I am sorry I wasted your time and part of your life. I did and do love you, I guess I was so broken that I could not show you properly and in the way that you deserved. I hope you find a real woman who will always love you, honor you and cherish you and does not have any baggage that will hinder your relationship. I was just not strong enough, I'm sorry.
I love you!

Goodbye,
Tina

I got back in the car and started going up and down the streets again. I was trying to figure out the timeline for when the email was sent. But how was it sent because it came in at a certain time, and you weren't home at that time? So, you had to send it from somewhere else. I went to the library, and the lady there remembered you. We looked at the cameras and saw you were in there. It showed when you came in and when you went out. At that point, it was, like I said, panic and fear. It was the thought of not running out of time. I needed to find you and talk to you. To find you and bring you back.

It had started getting dark; I remember sitting on the living room couch, just sitting there. Then, at one point, Jas came downstairs and sat next to me for a while. It wasn't a good night. It pretty much was a sleepless night. Your cousin or mentor called me back to see if we had found you yet. I said, "No, we still don't know anything." They then asked if I had checked your grandmother's house. "Yes, I sent the kids over there to look, and they didn't see anything. Nothing was moved or out of place to look like anyone had been there," I responded.

She inquired, "Did they not go inside the house? Because I feel like that's where she is."

"But the keys. The keys are here," I stated. Just then, the Holy Spirit said, "Go look at the key ring." I got off the phone and went to look. I guess we had been over there before, going in and out, trying to clean the house—that I knew what the keys looked like. When I went back to check the key ring, the key was gone. When I looked at it before, I didn't notice it; all that I saw was everything sitting on the dresser—the keys, the phone, and the rings. I had not focused on the keys. But when she said that, and I heard the Holy Spirit say look, I actually looked at the keys. I noticed that specific key was missing.

The key to get into Addie's house was a certain shape, and it was missing. In my mind, I replayed them, saying nobody had been there. Everything was locked and fastened. So, in my mind, if everything was locked and fastened and I thought the key was still there, you had not been there. I was up early because I had barely slept. I was moving with more intentionality then because I knew the key was missing, and I was going to Addie's house to go in and look for you. I had the second key, so I knew yours was missing. I had to wait for our two youngest to leave for school so as not to upset them. As soon as they were off, I jumped into the car. I didn't ask Jas or Malcolm to come with me, but they refused to go to school or work until we found you—they jumped in the car with me.

I drove quickly to get there. I jumped out of the car, went to the back of the house, unlocked the door, and went in. As I entered, I started looking for you. They were right behind me. I knew that if you were in the house, you would be in a room. So, my steps were heading toward the rooms. When I got there, I remember pausing. After I paused, they came up right behind me, almost running into me. And then, in that instant, it was a relief that you were there. But then, fear. Fear that I didn't get there in time. That's when I walked over to you. It started off as a soft shake to not startle you if you were asleep. Then, it went to a more aggressive shake because you weren't responding. "God, she is not responding."

Chapter 15

The Resolution
Mrs. Christina LaDonna Aydelotte

But God will redeem me from the realm of the dead; he will surely take me to himself. -Psalm 49:15 (NIV)

Be it resolved that Dr. Mark and Lady Lisa Jones, and the partners of The Center for Manifestation are in deep sympathy with the Aydelotte family in the passing of their loved one. Our hearts are with our beloved partner, John Aydelotte, and the Aydelotte family.

The death of a loved one can shake us to our very foundation. But, whatever the nature of your relationship with the beloved, we can pause today and give thanks to God for having the privilege of sharing life with her. We can remember that each of those memories and experiences was a gift from God. As Ecclesiastes 3:1 states, "To everything there is a season, and a time to every purpose under the heaven: A time to be born and a time to die."

This was almost my story and almost my resolution for my family - BUT GOD! Yes, I did take the pills, and yes, I did drink the gin in the Burger King cup. That day was to be the last time that I would have had to deal with the pain and suffering. I was almost "outta here." Barely conscious, barely breathing, and not responding when I was found – at first. But God.

John held me as I went in and out of consciousness. He took a quick glance up to look at the kids' faces. Malcolm and Jasmine were in the room with him. They were stunned. To walk into the room and find me lying unconscious and seeing the bottle of pills and the gin bottle on the floor scared them. But then I finally responded. I remember looking up and telling God, "I told you not to save me this time." A silent tear fell, and I passed out again.

John was so happy to find me still alive. He still doesn't remember who he called first: 911 or my mentor. Either way, thankfully, 911 was called, and I was taken immediately to the hospital to have my stomach pumped and stabilized. John called Apostle Mark to let him know they found me and to thank him and those who had been praying. As he was on the way to the hospital, all he could do was thank God that I was still alive.

Truly, the prayers of the righteous availeth much. And God said it was not finished yet. Even in my ignorance, God did not leave me. He had plans and purpose for me, and no devil in hell coming against me would interrupt His plans for my life. Not even me - He didn't let me get in my own way either.

To be honest, I don't know if I really wanted to die or if I felt that it would be easier to die and not have to deal with all the pain and suffering that I had gone through. Not to mention being told constantly that I was "nothing" and "weak." Fighting to get better seemed worse than just giving up altogether - fear of trying and failing. Let's be honest, even fear of succeeding. When trauma is all you know, then trauma is all you know.

Some will understand, and some won't. When you are in agonizing pain, whether physically, mentally, or emotionally, and there is no relief and all you want is for it to be over, your mind and those negative thoughts become larger than life. You feel alone, like no one truly understands. "They may sympathize with or feel sorry for me, but they don't feel the hell I am going through day and night. It would be better if I were not here, and they don't have to watch me being tormented day after day." These are the thoughts that go through the minds of those who have attempted and or successfully committed suicide. We don't want to suffer anymore, and we don't want our loved ones watching us suffer and not being able to do anything about it.

In my mind, I was a burden to my husband and my family, and because of that one more incident, I was done, and for me, it was over. But for my husband, it wasn't. He looked for me and prayed that I would be okay. He knew that if he could just talk to me, then things would be better. Same scenario but two different mindsets and perspectives. I was ashamed and embarrassed afterward. I just knew this was going to be the end, and I would never see him again. Now, I had to face him. I had to explain the unexplainable. Initially, I refused his visit while I was in the hospital. I know that seems harsh and wrong, but trying to wrap my mind around what had happened and then give him an explanation was too overwhelming.

That may seem selfish, but as a survivor (and now an overcomer), it doesn't feel selfish in those fragile moments. After having done the work, still doing the work, and talking with my family and those close to me, I could see how some might see it that way. Understand that, at that moment, being called selfish was not what I could hear or wanted to hear. I had to heal, get better, and get past those things that were holding me hostage and tormenting my mind. I needed help; I could no longer do it alone. I had to be honest about what was going on in my mind and my past. No more sugar-coating it, sweeping it under the rug, and remaining silent. All that did was bring me closer to a coffin that was going to be placed six feet underground.

Things didn't change overnight, but they did eventually change. We all had to work through the pain and trauma of that day in our own way. Everyone felt something different. I went to the mental hospital for about a week after the incident. They wanted to make sure that I was stabilized and had a treatment plan. I was put on medication, and I had to see a therapist weekly. I was nervous about going home and seeing my family. I definitely did not want to go back to church. What were their thoughts? Did they hate me now? Of course, my husband did his best to assure me I was loved and wanted at home, but I was still a little leery. This was a part of me facing my fears and those thoughts in my mind that were not true.

Coming home after leaving the hospital was challenging. I had to confront my children and face life head-on. After all, I had desired death, and it did not come for me. Well, it did, but God had other plans. For weeks, I felt like I was walking on eggshells, being ever so careful not to do or say the wrong things because tension lingered in the air. You could feel it, just as you can feel the rays of the sun on your face and the heat it brings. You can't touch it, but you know it's there.

I took baby steps as I began to re-engage with my family and work on my therapy. John didn't rush me; he remained by my side, encouraging and loving me through my process. Even when he didn't understand, he just prayed and stayed by my side. For a while, he became my security blanket. When we went out, I was right under him, and if I felt overwhelmed or scared, I would grab hold of him tightly. He would give me an ever-so-gentle squeeze back and say, "It's okay. I am here." I would then begin to calm down. It reminded me of when I was going through things, and I would lay on my mommy's lap and cry. She would stroke my hair and say, "It's okay. I'm here," and "It's going to be alright." Afterward, she would get quiet for a while. I realized later it was in the silence that she was praying over me. Now, it was my husband who was my comforter and prayer warrior.

Eventually, I had to have tough conversations with my children. It was not easy admitting to them that their mother failed and was ready to give up and leave them. They were hurt, of course, but the love I felt during those difficult conversations was indescribable. The negative thoughts told me *They hate you!* and *They will not want anything else to do with you.* More lies in my mind that had been made up to make me feel worthless and unloved. Having those hard conversations and using the techniques that I learned in my therapy sessions helped me to begin my healing process and move forward. Broken relationships were repaired, not just with my children but with others as well. Not every relationship was mended; some were meant to stay as they were. Toxic and abusive relationships are not to be repaired unless the other person is earnestly and actively participating in their own therapy on their own road to recovery. People can change if they choose to, but wisdom and time will tell you if they have changed for the better or if it is all an act.

It was about a month before I officially returned to church. I felt nervous about what people might think of me. I didn't know who was aware of my situation and who wasn't. I was nervous that information about my suicide attempt may have spread around the entire church. That fear stemmed from my past experiences. I had confided in someone about my personal struggles, seeking help at a previous church. Unfortunately, that person decided to share my story, and it spread like wildfire, including to the person I had the issue with. This only worsened my situation, and when I confronted them, they claimed it was framed as a request for prayer on my behalf. "Lies! You were gossiping and got caught," I exclaimed. I walked away, shutting down and avoiding sharing anything with anyone. People would look at me, engage in conversations out of earshot, or stop talking when I approached. I began to doubt who I could trust, so I chose silence.

I wasn't eager to go through that again, so I stayed away from church for a while longer. When I eventually returned, what I had feared and expected didn't happen. I wasn't criticized, ridiculed, shamed, or talked about. Instead, I was welcomed back with love and warmth. People had missed me and were genuinely happy to see me. The scenarios playing in my mind were far from the actual reality. The entire church didn't know what had happened. That was the fear talking. I needed to stop living in my imagination and embrace the present reality.

God knows what we need and when we need it, even if we don't realize it. For therapy to be effective, I had to actively participate. I had to be honest about my past experiences—the molestation, the feelings of rejection and abandonment from both parents, and the pursuit of love through unhealthy relationships, all while still feeling empty inside.

I didn't know what balance was or even how to set boundaries and standards at first. I just wanted to be loved and affirmed, so unfortunately, I put up with a lot of things that I should not have. Allowing people to talk to me any kind of way, using me to get what they wanted or get their job done.

My biological father was not in my life as a solid foundation nor to provide that love or affirmation for me to know or understand my worth. I desired that from him. If my own father left me and didn't love me (because that is what I thought), then how could anyone else? Daddy Thee came into my life stable as an adult. My foundation was already damaged. He did his best to love me and be there for me. And when I was shown love or the appearance of love because of what I was doing, I kept doing whatever that or those things were to keep receiving what I thought was love. There were times I didn't want to continue having sex, buying things, being talked to any kind of way, and doing extra, but if I wanted to feel loved, I had to keep doing it. Even in regular friendships or relationships, I tried to please them so they would stay my friends. Not wanting to rub them the wrong way by disagreeing with them or challenging them. So, I became who I thought they wanted me to be just to fit in their circle. Brokenness will cause you to go further than you desire to, all for the sake of feeling loved and valued.

Being abandoned and rejected by not just one parent but both was hard. My mother left me and went to live her life as if I didn't exist; at least, that is how Addie told the story. I saw other kids with at least one of their parents, and here, I had neither. It was hard to explain why the grandmother was raising me and not my mom or my dad. I made things up because the story was better than real life. But even when I told this made-up story—whatever it was at the time—my heart was always in pain because I knew the truth. They left me and went on with their lives. I had no parents to help me navigate who I was supposed to be, and I had to be okay with that. I became the great pretender, pretending to be who others wanted me to be because I didn't know who I was.

Due to some of the abuse and toxic relationships, I started to label all relationships as a lost cause. Coming from an abusive childhood makes one grow up feeling worthless and void of dignity. While I agree that using a light belt to spank your child for disobedience can be appropriate, it can also easily become abusive. I was yelled at, cussed out, then made to strip butt naked, had my hands and feet tied and then made to lay across the bed all while being beaten with an extension cord, which is definitely not appropriate. And it happened too many times to count.

Mentally, beatings like this break your self-worth. The beatings physically and mentally by my grandmother set me up, I believe, for the abusive and controlling relationship that I got into. He controlled so much of my life. Where I went, who I spoke to, what I did or didn't do. If I didn't obey MX or messed up (as he saw it), I was emotionally, sexually, or physically assaulted.

The abusive intimate relationship that I had gotten myself into led to the rape and the conception of another child. Though the conception was not favorable, I wouldn't abort my child, no matter the circumstances. When I did get the strength to leave MX and all his drama, I became homeless. Being homeless with one of my children while the others stayed somewhere else did something to my mind. It was torture, but what was worse was having to watch my son experience homelessness and act as if he was fine. Dealin with all these traumas, seeing things that others did not seem to see, but knowing they were there and real. Along with thoughts of suicide and worthlessness did not help me at all over the years.

I was drowning and needed help. I knew I had someone to help me, but at first, I didn't fully trust him, not really.

I had to help me, and that meant no more lying to myself or my therapist. Having gone through all of what I did, you learn to wait for the other shoe to drop. I prayed for genuine, good, true people and a great man, but when I was blessed with their presence, I waited for them to use me, abuse me, and cause me pain too. Because of my "stinking thinking," I set a chain of events in play to cause the downfall of relationships or run away from them when I got scared.

One of the things that I am remorseful about is not staying consistent with the therapy that my children needed. They went here and there. Looking back, they needed therapy just as much, if not more, than I did. We cannot forget about our children as we go through things. They are watching and going through as well. They can't comprehend the magnitude of what is happening.

> *As you prepare for this reflection section, sit and evaluate how you are feeling right at this moment. This chapter may have caused some triggers in your emotions. Don't sweep them under the rug.*

Resolve- Reflection

> *For I know the plans I have for you," declares the Lord, "plans to prosper you and not to harm you, plans to give you hope and a future. - Jeremiah 29:11(NIV)*

This one was heavy. Take a moment to process how you are feeling right now. What stands out in your mind? Have you been in this place? Are you there now?

Do you know of anyone who might be struggling with depression or suicidal thoughts? Do you know anyone who has gone through or is currently experiencing any of the areas we discussed? Were your words to them helpful or hurtful? If this person is you, and you have attempted to reach out for help, were the words that you received helpful or hurtful?

Chapter 16

Getting Help

There is nothing wrong with asking for help. Acknowledging a need makes way for provision. I had to learn this powerful principle the hard way. I told myself and others so many half-truths that I lost touch with the reality of my condition. Omitting certain things is still lying because you are not presenting the whole truth or the entire scenario required for healing and improvement. True, raw honesty has to come forth. It is the only way to confront the lies, destroy them, and build a genuine resolve. The thoughts swirling in my mind had become my reality, even though much of it was not true. I was living in my own personal bubble—a warped one, but a bubble, nonetheless.

Identifying your self-worth is crucial. Self-worth is not determined by your parents or their background, your associations, your financial status, or the type of job you hold. It is the internal sense of being good enough and worthy of love and belonging. This is something you must know and believe for yourself; no one else can do it for you. It's easy for us to believe criticism and negativity from others, but it is challenging to accept praise and esteem. The ultimate goal is to understand your self-worth; whether others put you down or lift you up, their words won't matter. I had to learn that, and I am still learning some days. No more emotional roller coasters because someone liked or disliked me or approved or disapproved of something I did or didn't do.

Healing is not a race; it is a journey. Take your time and learn to enjoy the process. I had to. I wanted everything to be over quickly—to take away the pain, the hurt, the anger, the fear, and all the negative feelings. Boom, it's over. The depression is gone, the feeling of worthlessness gone, the suicidal thoughts gone, the family dysfunction gone, the generational curses and cycles gone. No more abandonment, no more rejection, no more comparison, no more feeling guilty, no more feeling dirty from being molested and raped—just no more. All these things are traumas, but we can heal and overcome them.

Life doesn't work that way, sadly. Trauma and its effects and residue don't just dissipate. It's a process, a long one, but it's worth it. When we were born, we didn't come out walking and talking. We had to learn to turn over, scoot, crawl, and eventually walk—later, we learned to run. Each phase was not always easy and definitely not quick, but we got there. Retraining our minds to think differently from toxicity and negativity takes time. Learning to love the new you will take time, but it is so worth it.

Suicide and attempted suicide do not just affect the lives of the individuals committing the acts; they also impact their families and those who know and love them. If you know someone suffering from depression, watch for signs such as increased withdrawal, persistent sadness, lack of focus, increased distraction, missing important dates and deadlines (out of their nature), and constantly claiming everything is fine when you sense otherwise. If they express thoughts of others being better off without them or a desire for it all to be over, or even mention passing thoughts of suicide, don't dismiss them. Please don't write it off as a bad day or a passing moment. Listen, ask questions, and be understanding, even if you don't fully comprehend. A listening ear can make all the difference.

Help them by guiding them to professional help. I implore you not to belittle them or make them feel worse. You may not understand their struggles, but someone does. One simple gesture of kindness can change the course of someone's life.

Every 45 seconds, someone, somewhere, loses the battle and commits suicide. I had a champion fighting for me. His love, prayers, and support helped me recover and get the help I needed to become an overcomer. Now, I am part of the fight to help others.

When trauma is all you know, then trauma is all you know. Shift the narrative so trauma no longer needs to be all that you know, experience, and live from. Rewrite your story. Get help. And Live. Don't allow the traumas of your past to imprison your future. It's time to get unlocked.

Trauma Free - Reflection

Is there any area in your life you have been avoiding seeking counseling? Are you ready to take the necessary steps to seek help, undergo counseling, be honest, and embark on your healing journey? What will you do differently now to obtain the help you need to become a healed and whole person? If you have a loved one or a friend dealing with any form of trauma, what steps will you take to support and encourage them?

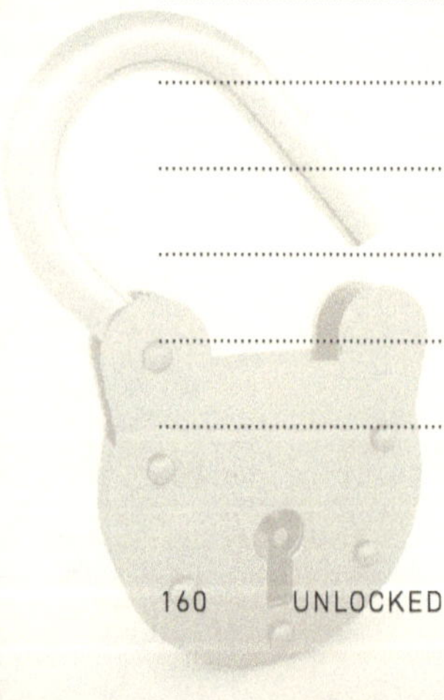

Change the narrative. How will you rewrite your story? Who do you desire to be? Nothing can stop you except yourself. I believe in YOU! Now it's time for you to believe in yourself!

You are fearfully and wonderfully made.
You are worthy and deserving of a whole and healed life.

Affirmations

I am worthy!

I am valuable!

I am whole, healed, and delivered!

I am loved, loveable, capable of love, and worthy to be loved!

I am forgiven; therefore, I will forgive myself!

I am fearfully and wonderfully made!

I am unique and will not compare myself to others!

I am an overcomer! Nothing is going to stop me.

I am not hopeless! I am hopeful in all things!

I have a divine purpose, and my life has meaning!

I will not fear failure or success! I will continue to move forward.

I am strong and confident!

I will not fear! Because God did not give me the spirit of fear but of power, love, and a sound mind.

I am strong and courageous!

I am rich beyond measure!

I am not alone; God is with me every step of the way! I will not fear.

Resources For You or Your Loved One

https://www.psychologytoday.com/us/therapists
https://therapyforblackgirls.com/
https://www.melaninandmentalhealth.com/
https://www.betterhelp.com
https://findtreatment.gov/
https://www.growtherapy.com

Suicide and Crisis Lifeline - Dial or text 988
National Suicide Prevention Lifeline - 1-800-273-8255

www.ingramcontent.com/pod-product-compliance
Lightning Source LLC
Chambersburg PA
CBHW050847150626
46549CB00012B/587